Changing Perspectives in Educational Research

David K. Wiles

The Ontario Institute
for Studies in Education

Charles A. Jones Publishing Company
Worthington, Ohio

1 2 3 4 5 6 7 8 9 10 / 76 75 74 73 72

Library of Congress Catalog Card Number: 77-181379
International Standard Book Number: 0-8396-0009-7

Printed in the United States of America

Preface

For those who want greater understanding and knowledge about educational research, its foundations and applications, *Changing Perspectives in Educational Research* is addressed to the many responsible for performing research and to those who are responsible for applying research findings.

The purpose of the book is twofold. It is to promote general understanding of a thinking process common to both research and daily educational decisions. It also is to show the firm connection between educational research and practice.

The book explains specifically how that thought process can be used in educational practice and how it is used in educational research. It will aid the person who wishes a pattern for logical thinking, the practicing educator who wishes to understand research without necessarily becoming an expert, and the student who needs a basic knowledge of research as a foundation for more study. In addition, it should help the university professor demonstrate the related nature of research and teaching or administration.

Chapter 1 outlines the crucial partnership between the practitioner and the researcher. Part 1 (chapters 2-4) presents directed thinking, the practitioner-oriented use of the common thought process, and describes it from practical, philosophical, and political viewpoints. The appendix gives a case study of its actual application to an educational issue.

Part 2 (chapters 5-12) presents scientific inquiry, the researcher-oriented use of the process. Chapter 5 demonstrates the similarities between directed thinking and scientific inquiry. Chapters 6-12 consider the application of scientific inquiry in the formal process of educational research.

I am indebted to the many friends and colleagues who encouraged and helped me in this task. Special acknowledgment is due Dr. Kimball Wiles who provided the major impetus for the writing and to my wife, Marilyn, for continued support during the writing of the book.

To Dr. Glen Fincher, Dr. Fred J. Brieve, Dr. Charles M. Galloway, Dr. John J. Kennedy, Dr. Don R. Logan, Dr. Stephen B. Lawton, and others who reviewed this material, I express appreciation for the insightful comments and suggestions made during preparation of both the practical and methodological parts of the manuscript.

David K. Wiles

Contents

Part One
Directed Thinking

1

The Researcher
and Practitioner
Partnership in Education

In the 1970s the relationship between research and the rest of the educational enterprise is far different than in past decades; research has moved from the periphery to the very core of the educational process. *Research has established itself as a primary vehicle by which change is promoted and effected in education.* Research has a major impact on the focus, direction, and development of all aspects of education. Innovations which are not the output of funded research or development projects are certainly an exception to the general rule today. In curriculum and instruction, such changes as the employment of the Physical Science Study Committee (PSSC), The School Mathematics Study Group (SMSG), and Computer Assisted Instruction (CAI) were founded in research endeavors. The open-plan concept and module-component subsystem, which have drastically affected thinking about what a school building is and should be, are research products. Other examples of research as a major force in the educational-change process cover such diverse areas as group process, organizational arrangements, and budget. Today, the central role of research in educational change is so familiar that it is often taken for granted, and it is hard to remember that a decade ago this was not the case.

Ten to twenty years ago educational research was all but separated from educational practice in the schools. Research seemed to belong to the people who worked at the periphery of education; the charge that research had little impact on actual educational practices had considerable merit. In 1960 less than *one-half of one per cent* of all people who would be considered "educationists" could be called researchers. (1).* Training for research in education reflected its subordinate role in the total enterprise: of all the universities and colleges in the United States only ten to fifteen had any planned program in educational research. A 1954-64 study of education graduates who had earned the doctorate found that nearly seventy-five per cent of them had not published any research ten years after receiving their degrees (2). From the perspective of today's academic marketplace, with latent pressures of "publish or perish" in refereed journals stressing empirical evidence, the fact that only one-fourth of Ed.D. or Ph.D. graduates were engaged in research publication seems incredible. Certainly it indicates strongly the shift in the present-day educational world.

The cause of the great shift in the relationship of research to education can be traced to a number of factors occurring in the early and mid 1960s. The United States and its World War II allies were shocked from their complacency about education and their view of the world community by the Russian launching of Sputnik in 1958, and an era of critical re-examination and compensatory reaction began. Many observers point to the election of John F. Kennedy and to his dream of the New Frontier as an example of the renewed vigor and energy exhibited at that time in western societies. Education came under especially sharp attack. The idea that the U.S.S.R., commonly thought of as one step removed from an "underdeveloped nation," could lead the race for space was seen as a direct result of educational mismanagement in the United States. The cold war spread to education. As early as 1960 the U.S. federal government had made substantial steps in counteracting the Sputnik shock. Two of the most important moves were to establish the Cooperative Research Program through the Office of Education and implement the titles of the National Defense Education Act. In both these moves to upgrade education the implication was clear; *research* was to spearhead the new educational drive. Nicholas A. Fattu noted in 1960,

> when the history of educational research is reviewed with the perspective of the future, these federal programs will probably stand out as the significant turning points in educational research (3).

The federal government's reaction also brought a cross-fertilization of many academic disciplines to education. Generally,

---

*Numbers within parentheses refer to Notes at the end of the book.

until the 1960s the behavioral, physical, and social-science disciplines were considered to be separate from education. Educators were perceived as a breed distinctly different from political scientists, sociologists, economists, philosophers and, as we have seen, researchers of all sciences. In the universities, courses such as politics of education (if offered) were taught by academics who were political scientists first, educators by guilt of association only. Educators were supposed to "educate" but certainly not meddle in the science of studying a particular behavior. By the same token, researchers who did work in education before Sputnik, either had primary allegiance to another academic discipline or were rare mavericks indeed.

Federal funds helped alter people's concepts about education. The emphasis on research caused many traditional educators to pick up research skills. Training programs in universities and in the field—in the school systems themselves—began upgrading the priority of research development. People in other academic disciplines perceived the funding direction for the future and began to integrate their specialties into the field of education. Change in the concept of education continues today. For example, many, if not most, current educational courses reflecting behavioral emphasis are taught by academics who majored in education. At this juncture, there seems no logical reason why the trend of educational supremacy and the subordination of other disciplines will not continue throughout the 1970s. In research, the trend means the researcher is engrossed in the educational process and an integral part of it; the researcher is an educator who differs from the practitioner only by his particular set of skills.

In the United States the research emphasis of the 1960s went through two general stages. We have noted how the initial funding stage brought about critical research interest and commitment to education. The second stage then focussed the research emphasis, helping to delineate what research would mean for the educational enterprise. The beginning of the focussing stage, which is truly responsible for moving research to a central role in the change process, can be traced to the Elementary and Secondary Education Act (ESEA) of 1965. The act was the most dramatic and far-reaching evidence that the federal government would use research as a means of improving education. In addition, the act gave notice that improvement would mean more than "pure" or invention-oriented research. While specialists were still encouraged to research for totally new ideas, concepts, and practices, there was also emphasis upon workers in development and dissemination; many researchers in education were now placed in direct contact with the field, carrying out development and dissemination roles. David Clark sums up the impact of ESEA and, by inference, the focus of research in education:

> The newly initiated efforts involved public schools, state education agencies, inter-agency organizations, community health and welfare programs, as well as the researchers in the college and university setting. A "tight little island" was no more. The educational research community was cracked open into a R and D component of the *social process* of education (4).

The federal mandate was now complete: Educational research would emphasize social or practical application. Development and dissemination functions stressed the use of research in practical, on-going educational situations. The partnership between researcher and practitioner was now crucial in order to meet the objectives and goals of education.

The reaction of the field to the changing role of research during the last half of the 1960s was interesting. Education is delegated to the various states by the 10th Amendment, and states have traditionally given the education function to the local community. The federal government has generally exerted influence in education through indirect means; funding has proved to be one of the most effective. The Elementary and Secondary Education Act of 1965 demonstrated the ability of the federal government to change the direction of education. After initial reluctance, the various state and local agencies actively sought federal funds that had research stipulations. The extent to which the research emphasis was accepted can be observed in the reaction of the field when federal money tightened at the end of the decade. Many specific products of research faced early extinction but the fundamental mechanisms for the conduct and use of research were maintained, and today large school systems have research and development specialists to assist in operations of the educational program. Most colleges and universities now offer a mandatory research course for the master's degree, whether M.Ed. or M.A. This also has significance for the field because promotion in many school systems is influenced by the extent of post-undergraduate education an applicant has. The point seems clear that research will continue to be a focus of change and improvement for education in the 1970s.

The meaning of educational research

The precise definition of research has eluded many brilliant scholars, including researchers who are attempting to describe their own educational role. One well-known researcher gave the honest if not clarifying description that educational research appears to be what educational researchers do (5). Another noted researcher, Julian C. Stanley, sums up the confusion:

> Vaguest of all is the word "research," which indeed means almost anything the educational user wishes, from asking a stranger his name to comparing the effect of polio vaccine with that of a placebo. "Research" has such a respectable sound that it is often used to dignify trivial or irrelevant activities (6).

Systematic attempts at definition have focussed on type of involvement, type of function, and general purposes of research. Researchers have been differentiated in terms of involvement as hard core, occasional, and monitors. Hard-core people spend a significant portion of their professional time in research or development activities; occasional researchers work from time to time on a project but the primary focus of their professional life is outside research activities; monitors maintain some communication with the research community through professional organization affiliation or subscription to research-oriented publications. These educators normally view themselves as consumers of the products of research rather than actual producers.

Researchers can fulfill a wide variety of functions depending on the purpose of their endeavors. They can be inventers, bookkeepers, engineers, evaluators, public relations men, trainees, or systems-maintenance personnel. Research functions are often divided into research, development, and diffusion categories but there is some overlap of functions in most classification schemes of this type.

Under the broad definition, educational research is oriented to five purposes: discovery of new knowledge, documentation and synthesis of knowledge, operationalization of found knowledge, testing and evaluation of knowledge, and dissemination of new information. Figure 1 outlines these research purposes in more detail.

It is doubtful if any one researcher would attempt to meet all the purposes described above. The task is too great and educational research is so complex that specialization dictates emphasis in a smaller number. Researchers usually specialize in either pure research, development, or the diffusion function. Inventers are normally concerned with the discovery and advancement of new knowledge, but there are three different types of inventers. Those who focus on

Figure 1　　Purposes of Educational Research

1. Discovery of new knowledge
    a. of the social and behavioral sciences
    b. of the educational process
    c. of operational problems

2. Documentation and synthesis of knowledge
    a. for the social and behavioral sciences
    b. for the educational process
    c. for the operationalization of information to the field

3. Operationalization of knowledge
    a. to translate conceptual information into operational terms
    b. to structure information into operational programs and packages

4. Testing and evaluation of knowledge
    a. of discovered information
    b. of operational information

5. Dissemination of knowledge
    a. to make field aware of new information
    b. to convince field of the value of information
    c. to train the field in the use of information
    d. to institutionalize the use of information (7)

advancement of knowledge for the social and behavioral sciences may or may not see their results as relevant to education; the educational value of these researchers is their addition to the general base of knowledge derived from *scientific inquiry* (8). The second type of inventer discovers and advances educational knowledge, investigating problems which are drawn from the ongoing educational process. The final type of inventer discovers operational problems which occur in the application and use of research knowledge.

Some educational researchers fulfill a bookkeeping function by documenting and synthesizing new knowledge. "Bookkeepers" may also specialize by knowledge of social and behavioral sciences, knowledge of the educational process, or knowledge in the operationalization of information. An aspect of educational research which showed phenomenal growth in the late 1960s and is continuing into the seventies is the engineering function. "Engineers" are concerned with the operationalization of research knowledge for the educational enterprise, and they may be divided into two types: translators who convert research knowledge into practical information which is applicable and useful to the field of education, and other "engineers" who structure diverse pieces of research knowledge into operational packages and programs.

Educational researchers also function as analysts of knowledge. New knowledge is tested for validity by replication of the scientific inquiry which produced the new information. Operational-type testing of information uses criteria such as feasibility of application to the field and usefulness to practitioners.

Finally, researchers function as public relations men, trainers, and systems-maintenance personnel to disseminate knowledge to the field. The "public relations" of research consists of promoting the awareness of new ideas and the value of changing current practices to incorporate new knowledge. Researchers train practitioners in the use of new packages and programs and attempt to guarantee that the knowledge will obtain a fair trial period in the field. People have a natural reluctance to change their current practices, so training and some institutionalization of new knowledge is crucial for field acceptance.

The researcher and the practitioner

The global purposes and functions describing educational research may make the reader wonder if practitioner can be distinguished from researcher.

Until the last decade the concept of practitioner was very different from the idea of researcher. The practitioner was characterized as the classroom teacher, school principal, or tough-minded superintendent facing the real-life problems of the daily ongoing educational process. The practitioner relied heavily on experience and feelings gained from years of educating children. On the other hand, the researcher was normally pictured as the university professor whose abstract, sterile thoughts circled in the clouds of academia. But during the 1960s it became evident that similarities between the two kinds of educators far outweigh the differences. Practitioners use objectively based, systematic thinking in the daily job of educating children; researchers share the moral and practical concerns of education. The partnership of the sixties, fostered by federal funding, has grown into the normal relationship of the seventies.

Who are the present-day educators that blend research and practice?

Mrs. Wendell has taught third grade for fourteen years, and she is generally known as a highly successful teacher and educational leader. Last year Mrs. Wendell became concerned with ways to evaluate change in attitudes and values of children; as she taught "Man: Course of Study" for two years the problem of how to analyze change had become apparent. Mrs. Wendell felt students were more open and self-directing after the course but she desired other criteria to substantiate her feelings. Even after spending several nights in the library of a local university studying information on evaluation techniques Mrs. Wendell felt that her findings were inconclusive. On the basis of her need to understand the impact of her course, Mrs. Wendell applied for and received a small federal grant to analyze "Man: Course of Study."

Mr. Jackson was concerned about problems of noise in the open-plan school of which he recently had become principal. Until this year he had been administrator of the conventional type of school building, and he felt that his past experience of ways to deal with noise problems was inadequate. The open-plan school had, in addition to a new structural arrangement, new concepts of learning and teaching. Mr. Jackson asked and received help from personnel in the research and development (R and D) department of the central office of his school system. After analyzing the noise level and providing information on technical aspects of open planning, the R and D department suggested several ways to alleviate specific noise problems.

Dr. Rich of North Central University worked with improving the decision process of Alco County's administrative hierarchy. Upon the request of the county Dr. Rich analyzed differences in perceptions about what the current decision practices were and what the ideal decision structure would be; the information also served as the basis of a training program to build congruence of perceptions for people in the school system.

Dr. Colburn taught the basic research course for candidates of all graduate education programs. His own research background was of the "experimental" school and the research course stressed methodological techniques for doing research. Until recently, Dr. Colburn had taught only M.A. sections of students and his course was well received, but this year, as the result of a restructured graduate program, Dr. Colburn taught both M.A. and M.Ed. students. Two weeks into the course he was faced by a contingent of angry M.Ed. students who disagreed with the basic "doing research" purpose of the course, and who wanted emphasis on the consumption of research instead. Dr. Colburn's initial reaction was to state that learning the "doing" of research would inevitably transfer to the "using" of research, but now, a week later, he was not so sure of his response. The question of what to offer in a semester course for students who were on terminal programs was a real one; most of them would only take one research course during their graduate studies.

Should the information presented be specific to cover a few topics thoroughly or general and cover everything but in less detail? Should the goal be to train doers of research or consumers, or to attempt both objectives in the time available? Finally, should the instructor practice a direct manner of presenting information or the indirect approach, allowing students to examine critically and "discover" research?

Dr. Colburn faced the questions which plague all teachers by going to the students, and they spent a class period discussing the problem. Later, certain students with experience in educational practices formed a group who, with Dr. Colburn, worked out course objectives they considered relevant and meaningful to all parties. Dr. Colburn spent extra time restructuring the course, but he now felt that the interests of research *and* field were being served better.

Mrs. Wendell, Dr. Jackson, Dr. Rich, and Dr. Colburn are four examples of educators who blend a research and a practical orientation. Each educator has a different way of wearing the two hats, and with the exception of Dr. Colburn, would probably not consider himself a "researcher." The 1970s will find it increasingly hard to differentiate two separate categories of educators. The number of educators wearing both the hats of researcher and practitioner will grow while the number of purists or separatists will diminish. The development of research into the central change agent of education and the sharpening focus of research on use and application makes certain the continued mutual awareness and understanding.

Similarities between researchers and practitioners

Beyond the need for mutual awareness and understanding which is dictated by the educational enterprise lies a deeper, more fundamental reason for the researcher-practitioner partnership. There is a basic similarity between the thinking used in research and that used in many types of educational practices. The functions of discovery, reporting, making ideas operational, evaluation, and dissemination are the concern of all educators. A basic thought process is shared by both researchers and practitioners; it is *objective, systematic,* and *rational.* It is objective because it is impersonal and free from personal bias that may adversely affect an educator's thinking. It is rational because that impersonality is gained by reliance on intellect or reasoning rather than emotion. It is systematic because the thought process has a consistent character or direction; thinking follows a regular, predictable pattern.

A systematic way of thinking which stresses rationality and objectivity is the foundation of educational research and is also the basis for many daily decision-making practices of schoolmen. The difference between the researcher and practitioner who think in this manner is *one of degree rather than kind*. The laboratory technician and the first grade teacher may both be systematic, rational, and objective. The difference in how they address problems is generally the degree of formalization or structure in their thought process. Both attempt to control thinking procedures by certain guidelines which characterize a research-oriented approach. The researcher attempts to control the process by an elaborate external plan called a research design. The practicing educator attempts control by a series of internalized "rules" which direct his consideration of situations.

The thinking process of formal research is labelled *scientific inquiry*. It incorporates objective, rational, and systematic procedures which control and direct the formalized inquiry into a problem. These procedures are the generally agreed-upon criteria of "good" research. Part II of this text discusses these criteria in terms of defining problems, collecting information, and analyzing and interpretating data. Formal research, regardless of the extent of procedural "rules," still represents an attempt to control a person's thinking about a problem.

The practitioner who thinks in a rational, systematic, and objective manner shares the fundamental characteristics of scientific inquiry. However, the thought control usually takes a different form from strict scientific method when applied to practices in an ongoing school situation. The thinking becomes less formal, more internalized, and usually directed at one major problem with a series of interlocking subproblems. This practical modification of scientific inquiry is called *directed thinking*. Thought is directed by a series of internalized rules or guidelines by which a practitioner can check his perceptions when making educational decisions.

Directed thinking attempts to add another frame of reference to individual feelings by providing a set of specific thinking procedures. Everyone has certain preferences, dislikes, and opinions which color perceptions of an ongoing situation. This coloring is called bias, and it is a natural result of the particular set of experiences each person has had; although no two people can perceive a situation in exactly the same way or share identical biases it is fair to say that all people are biased. Thus bias is not a negative term but a consequence of being human.

All thinking is influenced to a great extent by a person's perceptions of the world. In fact, one school of psychology states that all personal reality is dependent on how an individual perceives a situation and *not* on what the observable facts are (9). This makes sense when reality is considered in terms of an individual *in* a situation rather than reality for the observer *of* a situation. A teacher may feel that her fifth period class is doing well, with learning going on and all the children happy, yet an observer in the back of the classroom may detect that half the children are disinterested or exhibiting nonverbal anger. Which is reality? In a sense, both are reality. Certainly the teacher's perceptions of the class are her reality no matter what the observer may discern.

Directed thinking is a process by which the practitioner checks perceptual reality. It provides a means of analyzing a situation by following criteria that are external to personal beliefs, values, and attitudes, and in this way to help resolve a variety of educational problems. Its practical application is nearly universal and educators can use directed thinking to help assess curriculum issues, administrative problems, discipline, political confrontations, lunchroom scheduling, or other school decisions.

Summary

Educational research has become a partnership between researcher and practitioner both of whom share the need for mutual awareness, understanding, and cooperation in the 1970s. Research is a primary change agent for the educational process. Educators will continue to coordinate their activities with research efforts because of governmental commitments to research as a vehicle for change. Both types of people will find similarities in their work because of a basic likeness in ways of thinking about educational problems. The scientific inquiry of researchers and the directed thinking of practitioners cement the crucial partnership by a rational, objective, and systematic means of making decisions.

Questions

1. Is cooperation and understanding between educational reseachers and practitioners imperative for the 1970s? Why?

2. In what context is educational research described by this text?

3. What are the general purposes of educational research?

4. Who are the "engineers" of research?

5. What are the characteristics of the fundamental research-oriented thought process shared by practitioner and researcher?

6. What is the relationship between directed thinking and a person's perceptions of the world?

2

Directed Thinking—
The Informal Process

Directed thinking can be best described as it influences the making of educational decisions. Decision-making can be divided into three stages: describing problem situations, testing an argument, and interpreting results (1). When describing a problem, the person involved collects information and makes predictions. The information may be facts, feelings, attitudes, or opinions about a situation; the predictions reflect a guess or argument about what is real or true.

Testing an argument consists of judging one prediction against all other possible explanations of reality. In other words, there is some standard or criterion by which predictions of reality are tested.

Finally, the person interprets how the results relate to some standard used for judging, explaining the outcome in terms of a specified situation. The interpretation now becomes information used in describing other situations, and we have made the complete circle in the thought process.

Although decision-making can be traced through three stages, there is a wide variety of forms which particular thinking processes may take. Different types of information may be collected and predictions may be made in a number of ways; the standard against which a person tests a particular argument or interprets results may range from personal feelings to a set of written regulations. Through the describing, testing, and interpreting stages, certain aspects of the thinking process distinguish directed thinking.

Describing the problem

The directed thinker describes a problem by defining an issue, making predictions, and collecting information.

Defining a specific issue to be resolved often is subject to bias that subsequently influences thinking. The language is filled with words which are commonly used but not understood: administrators are asked to act "democratically" with teachers; principals hear demands for more "sharing" in local school decisions. What do these words mean? A principal may speak of teacher participation while thinking of teachers acting in an advisory capacity, yet the staff may demand participation and be thinking of making final decisions. It is easy to envision a school situation where the problem of staff participation in decision-making is recognized, verbalized, but still not understood.

The directed way of thinking promotes a built-in systematic concern about meaning. Directed thinking stresses objectivity and rationality. The practicing educator who adopts this way of thinking must consciously consider his thought actions; he must think in words and concepts that can be described by concrete, observable matters. The directed thinker does not assume that people understand the words used to describe an issue, but asks that phrases and terms be defined in terms of the actual situation.

For example, a group promoting the "democratization" of education would be asked to specify their assumptions about the values of "democracy." What is necessary or what must occur to make education democratic? The assumptions about psychological attitudes, organization structure, and any other pertinent factors would be recorded, as would assumptions about the decision process necessary to insure the achievement of democracy.

Notice that this procedure does not place a value judgment on the actual definitions drawn by a particular group. If the group stated that democracy meant all teachers must vote on every school issue, this definition would not be judged good or bad, true or untrue. Directed thinking would only analyze the assumptions made and ask that the operations necessary to implement these assumptions be consistent. In effect, use of a standard to judge definitions permits us to understand the differences between the dictionary meaning of a word and the way it is actually used (2).

The importance of demanding concrete definitions of words and problems can be demonstrated in a number of practical educational situations. For example, many boards of education have had to face controversial issues surrounding the teaching of sex education; normally, subjective statements and personal opinions have run wild in the discussion. Many well-meaning members take dogmatic positions on the issue because the definition of what it means to "teach sex education" in a particular school system has not been agreed upon. Without agreement who can blame a religious person from interpreting sex education as immoral or some member judging the teaching as a subversive political plot to brainwash children? In a climate of emotional conflict a person is likely to base his arguments on what he knows best: his personal feelings, opinions, and bias.

Agreement on the meaning of words and the description of problems is a necessary step toward understanding among people. It adds the critical note of consistency which is necessary for solving problems in a rational manner.

Once a person describes an issue he makes guesses or predictions about the resolution, a crucial step in problem solving that has several implications for directed thinking. Many people give possible explanations without careful thought. A principal may predict that teachers do not want to participate in school-wide decisions because he did not want to when he was a teacher; again, subjective feelings determine how the person predicts the outcome of a problem. The directed thinker checks his personal feelings by building a rational means of testing the prediction. The crucial distinction between the directed-thinking process and the principal's subjective prediction is that in the former the guess becomes something to be tested rather than a statement of fact. Predictions which cannot be tested cannot be proved wrong, but unfortunately, much thinking in education treats predictions as though they were foregone conclusions.

A second implication of making predictions according to directed thinking is that more than one plausible explanation is usually identified. The educator must then rank each possibility as more or less probable as a prediction, thus allowing himself to return to other possible explanations if the original guess is rejected (3). On the other hand, subjective predictions are often singular and may be couched in language like "I'll bet my bottom dollar that. . . ." This orientation may increase a person's attempt to guarantee that the prediction is confirmed.

In collecting information about a problem, directed thinking requires adherence to a set of systematic rules that make the thinker accept information from all sources, even those that present ideas which are contrary to his prediction. A natural outcome of personal bias is to select only information which supports a particular view.

For example, a person who "knows" that "most poor children are delinquents" will view a ghetto situation in a biased manner and will select only information which supports his convictions. This approach to collecting information will, by the same selective bias, also rule out certain possible counter-predictions.

To summarize the method by which a problem is described, a person controls his bias by systematic rules in thinking. In describing a problem he must define an issue consistently by using words capable of being tested, words that represent concrete behavior or phenomena which can be observed. The description must make predictions based on information that has been collected objectively. Each prediction must be capable of test in order to show whether the guess is plausible or not. The best guess is selected from a number of possible predictions; once it is chosen, information is collected which will either substantiate the prediction or prove it untenable.

When an educational problem has been described in this directed-thinking manner, an issue is defined, a prediction is made, and information is collected. Now the person is ready to test his argument. For the directed thinker this means testing a specific prediction made about an issue's resolution.

Testing an argument

Testing has two aspects which differentiate directed thinking from other forms of thinking. First, the prediction that is being tested has a built-in chance of being rejected. A prediction in the form of "disadvantaged" children are "disadvantaged" is not acceptable in directed thinking — could an educator show that the people tested are anything but disadvantaged? If the criteria for testing are not part of the prediction's description there is no way to disprove it; a directed thinker must make his prediction in a form that can be tested; perhaps a person would be said to be disadvantaged if the score of 70 was made on a certain test. When a prediction is not capable of rejection as a result of testing, it becomes a self-fulfilling prophesy.

Second, testing also implies that the educator will follow a systematic procedure to analyze his argument. Returning to our prediction of disadvantaged, notice that for a valid assessment the child must make a certain test score to be classified: the procedures which the directed thinker uses to find the magical number and to analyze the level of acceptance for disadvantaged must be specified. There is good reason for this specification in thinking. Suppose another person disagreed that a certain set of scores indicated disadvantage. If the procedures for testing are specific the skeptical person may duplicate the test. The ability to analyze and duplicate the testing procedure is critical in directed thinking because it allows findings to be judged reasonable or not.

After a problem has been described and a prediction tested the directed thinker must still make conclusions and draw inferences in a cautious manner. The results of testing must answer questions about both the specific prediction and more general problems.

A prediction has either been demonstrated actually plausible or not. A child can be classified disadvantaged or he has some other test score. As long as the criteria for directed thinking were carried out in the describing and testing phases the interpretation of the specific prediction is self-evident.

Interpreting results

The crucial aspect in interpreting findings is generalization to the original problem from the outcome of testing the prediction. Once the specific prediction is shown plausible or false what can a person say about the general problem?

Directed thinking demands that an educator's inference be both logically consistent with the outcome of the prediction and tentative in nature. If the educator is logically consistent, he cannot make a generalized conclusion which does not fit the results of the prediction. A principal analyzes the attitudes of certain faculty members about serving on a committee to decide the color of new curtains, and the prediction that the teacher attitudes would be negative is borne out. An example of lack of consistency between the specific argument tested and the general problem would be a conclusion by the principal that teachers do not like to participate in local school decisions. The prediction pointed out negative teacher attitudes about a particular form of participation on a specific topic; the inferential leap to conclusions about participation in general is too great to be consistent. It does not fit the framework of logic.

A logical generalization in this example is that teachers cannot be assumed to want participation for participation's sake. Other specific questions about the aspects of decision-making in which teachers do want to participate and about how sharing is to be accomplished are still unanswered.

Finally, outcomes must be interpreted as tentative conclusions. One of the basic characteristics of directed thinking is relativity; there are no absolute answers or conclusions which are assumed true for all times.

Notice that the possibility of being wrong is provided for in several stages of the thinking process. When defining words we must specify a particular set of circumstances; the possibility that someone will assume that other circumstances are described by the same label always remains unless meaning is clearly specified. A correctly constructed prediction has built into it the test and the potential for being shown either plausible or not. Findings are interpreted by the standard of acceptability in the prediction. The process is deliberately formed so the thinker can never arrive at dogmatic or absolute findings (4).

To conclude, a directed-thinking practitioner must consider educational problems according to certain rules of thinking. In effect, a systematic procedure directs how a person describes, tests, and interprets a decision-making situation. Figure 2 illustrates the crucial points in controlling personal subjectivity during the thought process.

Figure 2   **Directed Thinking**

1. Describing an Issue
    a. Data collection objective
    b. Predictions testable
    c. Terms operationally defined

2. Testing an argument
    a. Error possibility recognized
    b. Procedures capable of duplication

3. Interpreting the outcomes
    a. Generalization logical
    b. Tentativeness

Practical uses of directed thinking

A description of thinking can make a person's thought process sound unambiguous, objective, and simple to understand, but in reality, thinking is complex. It is easier to describe thinking than to apply a thought process which follows standard guidelines. A description paints a static picture which the reader can analyze at arm's length; use of directed thinking means involvement in the on-going, dynamic situtation.

The educator may feel that the practical problems of time and effort could overwhelm the benefits of systematic thinking in schools, and he may conclude that the concept of directed thinking is in the "nice idea but not realistic" category. Educators in large city school systems which are beset by urban ills are particularly skeptical of thought processes which require objectivity and time for reasoned analysis of daily problems. Certainly a number of problems facing *all* educators can be classified as crisis issues; in these situations the educator will continue to make judgments much as a doctor does when treating a patient in a crisis. The time available and conditions may demand immediate action and the educator's experience may become the only resource for decision-making, but no educational system or person faces uninterrupted crisis situations over long periods of time (and survives). Although the teacher, principal, or superintendent on a Friday afternoon may feel like the past week was one continual headache there were probably periods of less than crisis conditions.

In these periods of relative calm or normal activity, directed thinking can add a valuable blend to subjective perceptions in making practical judgments. The charges of additional effort and time spent in problem-solving may have some validity, but the benefits seem worth the trouble when the possible consequences of a personal-inclination approach to thinking are considered. *Sole* reliance on past experience or guesses is becoming increasingly limited as a means of handling modern day educational problems, and it involves great risks if not checked by other criteria for making decisions. Ask the inner-city school administrator who tries to tell the local community that he knows what is best for their children. Ask the teacher who tries to tell teenagers what they want and need. A person can rely on his personal beliefs, values, and experience only up to a certain point; after the point is reached another basis for thinking must also be used or the results can be tragic.

The complicating aspect of directed thinking in education is that the natural and social contexts of decision situations form unique, multifaceted problems. For example, a problem of child intelligence often overlaps with social, economic, or ethnic problems. The outcome may become a political issue. Specific problems of a particular decision environment can not be listed as general issues. A major problem centers on the assumption that educational surroundings are similar. How many times do we read of an "urban" school or the "rural" school system? Yet even in the days of the one-room schoolhouse specific educational environments were dissimilar; in the United States a list of educational issues taken from a New England setting at the turn of the century could not be expected to match the specific educational problems found in the deep South or far West (5).

The same specific dissimilarities exist between the school systems of today's complex, shifting society. Broad ethnic, religious, and political problems are common but their exact forms at the local-school or central-office level are infinite.

In spite of differences, the educator can identify general similarities which will affect practical judgments. Broad similarities of this kind are discussed below.

Uncertainty

Today's practitioner can be sure of one factor in education; in many crucial arenas of decision making the number of certain or unquestioned decision procedures is diminishing rapidly. Making practical judgments is no longer a question (if it ever was) of relying solely on "the book," for organizational rules and regulations provide a diminishing number of procedures which are realistically accepted as applicable to certain crucial issues. More often, the educator must find out what a particular situation is before he makes any attempt at a decision.

For example, in the past the local school principal could make a large majority of daily decisions with a high degree of certainty, because the central-office and board policy stated what could and could not be done. Within the local school the authority of the principal was unquestioned. Teachers, students, and the local community recognized the fact that, in the final analysis, actual decision authority and power rested with him.

Today, in many places, the actual power of the principal has been changed radically (6). In certain cities, school-system rules and authority relations are determined by the board of education bargaining with teacher unions or powerful community-interest groups. Within the local school center the decision power of the principal is challenged by students, teachers, or the local community. The end result of these challenges to the principal's role and decision power is that he operates with a high degree of frustration and uncertainty.

Similar examples of uncertainty in making practical judgments could be given for teachers, superintendents, coordinators, or board members. Uncertainty seems to be a factor which the practitioner must grow to expect throughout the educational environment.

Complexity

The educational environment has become a highly complicated place to make practical judgments. Even at the classroom level the problems which the educator faces are intricate mixtures of many factors. The teacher must face large classes that often make impossible any situation which can approximate the close teacher-pupil relationship of the one-room-schoolhouse days, and his practical judgments may have to be largely based on the standardized test scores. Physical numbers and lack of time sometimes crush warmth and close interpersonal relations.

The complexity of education is reflected in the new curriculum. When the McGuffy Reader was in vogue a 6th grade teacher knew exactly what and how to teach; the subject and sequence were outlined; teaching became a matter of "plugging" students into the set curriculum. Today very few things are constant in curricula. The approach to teaching which consists of mastering one type of information at one rate of advancement is fading(7). Current curricula reflect recognition of many types of information (*e.g.* independent study) and many rates of advancement (*e.g.* continuous process, discovery learning). The teacher's role has become much more complex, for he must blend a number of factors affecting learning rather than just preaching "the true word."

Of course, examples of the growth of educational complexity could be demonstrated at other levels of the school system; the number of functional superintendents and central-office personnel needed to handle education in a large school system is staggering when compared to the central office role of the 1920s(8). The complexity of educational problem solving re-emphasizes the need for a systematic way of thinking.

Immediacy

Education reflects the hurry-up world of today's living. Time has become increasingly fluid and change more rapid, so that objects and ideas often become obsolete even before they are used or accepted(9). The immediacy of the current education scene has direct implications for practical decision-making. One is the constant demand for specific answers without time for reflection or proper analysis(10). The educator finds his job filled with the clamor for concrete, immediate solutions. Both the board member who receives a phone call from a citizen demanding action on some communication and the principal facing a group of angry teachers wanting student discipline enforced are feeling the impact of immediacy on making practical judgments. Many people demand point-in-time decisions on issues that have long-range consequences, yet quick judgments may be detrimental for they rule out possible alternative solutions which can only be developed over a period of time by more complete thought.

Competition

A final characteristic of education today is competition among forms of thinking. The interrelationships within the combined-science field of education cause the clash of many forms of ideas and ways of thinking. There are numerous different views of reality, and the educator must know which of them clash with directed thinking.

To summarize, the educational environment which affects practical judgments has four basic characteristics: uncertainty, complexity, immediacy, and competitiveness. These factors take different forms in specific issues but they can be expected to affect our perceptions of most day-to-day educational decisions.

Aids to judgment

Directed thinking involves at least the following four general considerations which help counteract the modern dilemmas of making practical judgments. Taken individually, the suggestions are not unique to the directed form of thinking, but taken together they force an educator to consider each aspect of an issue consciously and systematically. The specific controls and combined effect of all four considerations support the practical ability of directed thinking to handle realistic educational problems.

Setting priorities

To employ directed thinking, the educator must first identify decision areas where it is practical. Thus the first general consideration involves setting priorities. Every practicing educator has been told at one time or another to set priorities and specify goals to be accomplished, and in spite of the overworked and often trite nature of this phrase, setting priorities has a very practical meaning for directed thinking. It represents the blend between what the thinker wants to accomplish and what the realities of his situation dictate. It indicates a recognition that some issues or educational problems are more practical for directed thinking than others. Each educator must make a practical analysis of what problems are to be emphasized. As we have discussed earlier, directed thinking is not a personalized process; it can be used for analysis of any issue or objective, but it cannot be used to "prove" any idea because of the built-in chance of error. The educator must specify the issues or problems upon which he will use directed thinking, and to do this he must analyze both his personal values and the educational environment.

In a particular school situation a principal might think of a number of objectives or goals he would like to accomplish. He would like to balance the budget, improve staff development, encourage curriculum reform, involve community groups, and share decision-making with students, faculty, and the other school people concerned (11).

Against the list of what the principal would like to do he must set another list of what he can or must do. The local school budget must be in good form or the area superintendent will be unhappy. Although the current in-service program on curriculum is not going well, change in this area is not critical. The school recently was boycotted by students and community members demanding participation in decision-making. In this illustration, setting priorities may be pretty automatic; the solution of issues critical for survival in the principalship seems foremost. Most educators do not have these extreme choices, and priority setting becomes a matter of degree of emphasis between a number of possible goals. The foremost priorities are established by balancing personal inclination and situation feasibility.

Testing objectives

After the educator judges which decision areas are most applicable to directed thinking, his second general consideration must be to put his problems into testable form. The principal in our example would like to do such things as improving curricula or involving students in decision-making, but the directed thinker would not be able to make practical judgments about these objectives; he must think in terms of concrete operations which can be observed and tested. The directed-thinking educator cannot talk of solving the "lunchroom problem" or "student unrest" without further specification. What is to be accomplished must be specified clearly at the same time that priorities are chosen. The question of improving curricula must be defined in terms which will tell what "improve" and "curricula" mean. The testability of objectives lies in their description; the educator must specify how and when an objective will be reached.

Choosing the critical path

A third way directed thinking helps the educator make practical judgments is to force consideration of the most feasible way of accomplishing an objective. Once the objective is spelled out, the process of directed thinking compares the alternative methods of reaching the goal. The specific steps of the directed thinking process are stated in terms of prediction. The consideration of steps necessary for problem-solving by directed thinking compares the alternate solutions.

An example of finding the critical path to a practical goal may be seen in the teaching of world history. In many schools a teacher who judges that the easiest way to teach history is to follow the prescribed ten-year-old textbook without deviation is in trouble. To deny the impact of nationalism and growing ethnic identification on the content of history in the last decade is a sure invitation to disruptive controversy in some educational situations (12). The teacher who does not widen the scope of teaching beyond an outdated textbook may well flounder. In this case, the realities dictate that the process of going chapter by chapter, page by page is *not* the most feasible way to reach the goal.

The directed thinker who hypothesized a number of alternative ways to reach the goal of teaching world history would immediately see this error. The question of irrelevance would surely become a criterion for testing different methods of teaching. New information, analyzing nationalism and ethnic identification, would be incorporated into the selection process. Education is changing so quickly that processes for reaching goals must be questioned and analyzed like the objectives themselves.

Judging self and others

As a final general consideration, directed thinking helps an educator make practical judgments about himself and others in the social situation.

By systematically analyzing the assumptions and biases of other people on particular issues, directed thinking can be used to identify other forms of thinking present in that situation. Through a series of questions any form of thinking can be identified.

The directed thinker looks first to the value assumptions a person makes to frame his thinking. All of us carry about certain values inculcated by society and our personality; it is impossible to think outside a cultural context. The phrase, "we hold these truths to be *self-evident*," is an open declaration of a certain value framework for the United States, but the directed thinker cannot assume how a specific person interprets the professed abstract cultural values. For example, the right of and need for an "educated" citizenry *may or may not* be interpreted to mean compulsory training in a formal school institution (13).

The directed thinker must determine the general value framework a person takes at the most personal level. As the context become more concrete the directed thinker should be able to identify specific meanings which a person assigns to general value questions.

Secondly, the directed thinker should determine a person's specific values toward the thinking process. A particular individual may assume thinking should follow some outside criterion, should be an internal and emotional process, or should be a combination of these processes, depending on the problem. Each judgment tells a person's values about the thinking process.

The practicing educator who recognizes the differences in values about thinking may solve many school issues; conflicts in personal values frequently override any consideration of an educational issue. For example, an emotional teacher and a rationally-oriented teacher serving on a committee to judge the merits of the school art program might be expected to spend more time defending their own thought processes than considering the issue.

Finally, assumptions about conclusions should be determined. Often a thinker has a particular "stake" in the outcome of findings, which may be shown when results are presented with such words as "ought" or "should" being given without qualification. The directed thinker determines a person's assumptions about conclusions and places them on a scale between genuine prediction and flat prescription.

A thinker can judge his own value assumptions as well as those of others. By evaluating his value framework, thinking process, and conclusions, a person may objectively analyze his own assumptions.

A valuable outcome of judging ourselves and others in this way is the defensibility of our eventual position. The analysis procedure and built-in chance-of-error checks may keep an educator from adopting an indefensible position in thinking, and in extreme cases defense may well be crucial for survival. The practitioner knows that education today is often a rough-and-tumble world.

The actual attempt to be systematic and objective also puts a person in a particular thinking stance. The directed process demands that the user make and live with certain basic assumptions about reality, knowing, and thinking.

Directed thinking, like any other form of thinking, presents one view or "window" of reality. The questions of what is real and how do we know have troubled man throughout history; the major objective of comparative philosophy is to assess how people interpret reality and knowing. Brilliant teachers have answered the questions of how to find and recognize reality in many very different ways (14). The particular slant that an educator must take in directed thinking also colors certain of his interpretations and requires him to make decided assumptions.

Reality for the directed thinker

Reality is personal experience. Reality for the directed thinker is tentative and can be expected to change as the social situation changes. This means that the directed thinker has an inherent distrust of all labels which treat "facts" as constants. Unfortunately, much of the language and thinking in education is based on constants that are assumed to represent reality. Labels like slow learners, local school administrators, ghetto, union, continuous progress, and many others are applied to facets of education as fact. Because of this, the educator hears statements such as these which are expected to be taken as fact:

"Members of the teacher's union are militants"
"Residents of the ghetto hate school officials"
"Disadvantaged children are intellectually inferior"
"Local school administrators are authoritarian"
"Continuous progress is a failure"

None of these statements represent reality to the directed thinker because they all assume too much. Certain teachers may indeed be "militant," but can a person assume that all teachers belonging to the union must be militant? Can a person assume that all ghetto residents hate or all principals are authoritarian? Of course not. Reality for the directed thinker depends on the particular social situation at a point in time and at a given place.

After recognizing the relative and changing nature of reality in an immediate social situation, the educator can predict the state of reality in a future or general context. Perhaps the study of a situation finds that, in fact, principals do tend toward authoritarian controls or that students in continuous-progress curricula are failing to meet school expectations. Reality then becomes a matter of how secure a directed thinker feels in generalizing results to encompass a future or broader scope. He recognizes that prediction is a deliberate step *away* from the concrete reality in a specific situation, but he also knows that prediction is an educated guess and not a prescribed certainty. In this manner the concept of reality is extended beyond the strict description of the here-and-now.

How the directed thinker knows

Knowing depends on an internalized controlled process of thinking. The directed-thinking process emphasizes the relative nature of knowing; both the systematic steps and the rational orientation of the method attempt to provide a controlled method of assessing reality, but the process deliberately incorporates a degree of uncertainty which allows flexibility. The field of education has few, if any, constants to which a fixed process of knowing can be applied. Program Planning Budgeting System (PPBS) is an attempt (15). The relative nature of the thinking environment demands that educators use directed thinking as a guide or framework, but not as a prescribed commandment, for the thinking process used to find reality can be no more dogmatic than can judgment of the results be absolute. Both process and findings must be flexible enough to adjust to the constant modifications of problems in today's schools. Directed thinking is a process which blends the necessity of consistency with the recognition of uncertainty.

What the directed thinker assumes

The assumptions of directed thinking place an educator in a framework of certain stipulations, which some people may consider limitations to the scope of thinking. It is true that a controlled-thinking process, such as directed thinking, is limited, but any argument that another form of thinking may be limit-free is false. All thinking is controlled by being based on certain assumptions (16). In this sense, all thinking is limited. However, the educator does not lose his capacity to choose which limits, assumptions, and forms of thinking he will use in any social situation.

Directed thinking does not attempt to replace all other forms of thinking. In fact other forms, such as assumptions of faith and certain emotional convictions, have valid places in societal living (17). An educator must recognize and stand by the assumptions of directed thinking *only* if he chooses to use that particular form.

The directed form is based on certain assumptions about the framework, the actual process, and the findings of thinking.

The directed thinker must assume that all thinking or problem-solving is tentative and relative. The assumption of total relativity is hard for most people to accept; many people have religious, moral, or political convictions which they consider absolute. By conscious recognition of those areas we will not mistake directed thinking for some other form of thinking. When a person believes, without question, that God exists or democracy is the best form of government then he has gone beyond the directed-thinking approach and has identified unquestioned convictions that are outside the assumptions necessary for directed thinking.

This form of thinking also assumes a systematic, rational process of thinking. A directed thinker must follow logical consistency from explanation to prediction and must meet both the factual and testable criteria. Again, directed-thinking assumptions limit the thinker to a rational, systematic process, and eliminate emotional arguments or information. The statement "I know because I feel" could not be accepted as factual information no matter how strong its appeal. We all rely on emotional judgments at times; for example, love is based on feeling and emotion. Directed thinkers would have a person consciously recognize when he begins another form of thinking.

Finally, the directed thinker must generalize his findings in a social context. He must assume an obligation to infer to a larger context than the immediate situation and predict future social results. Simple description or prescriptions about what ought to be done in education are outside the directed-thinking process.

Questions

1. How is a decision problem described by the directed thinking process?
2. How are predictions tested through directed thinking?
3. How are findings or conclusions interpreted with directed thinking?
4. How does directed thinking help make practical decisions?
5. What is reality for the directed thinker?
6. How does the directed thinker know?
7. What must the directed thinker assume?

3

Comparing Directed Thinking to Other Forms of Thinking in Education

The practicing educator encounters various forms of thinking in the job of educating children. The teacher, principal, superintendent, and local-board member are bombarded by a constant interaction of different thought processes and values. Identifying specific forms of thinking is often a difficult task, but the practitioner may be assisted by some common, everyday indicators of different thinking frameworks (1).

The Teaching Function

The teaching function may demonstrate different forms of thinking in such specific aspects as classroom seating arrangements, teaching specialty and method, discipline, or evaluation procedures for students.

Seating students in alphabetical order may indicate that a teacher places high value on procedure and system (2). The teacher may consciously support the impersonality created by the seating if he feels that familiarity breeds egalitarianism and possible contempt. Another teacher may not care where students sit in the classroom and may not consider fixed seating an important prerequisite for learning and teaching. Personal values and preferences are frameworks for different forms of thinking, and therefore whether a teacher seats children in a certain order or is unconcerned about seating may show his values and thinking.

Different thought processes often underlie open controversies in education. For example, the grouping of students either heterogeneously or homogeneously for learning may become a philosophical issue.

Heterogeneity is supported by the argument that slower children need the stimulus of brighter pupils to help learning. Also, the argument for democracy is often invoked because segregation by intelligence or ability creates, by implication, a class distinction among students. The criteria for truly "separate but equal" education have proved elusive and difficult to apply in real-life situations.

Grouping children with like intelligence is based on the argument that students need special challenge and opportunity for individual success, and that they must be segregated into special classes to compensate for differences in native ability. Teachers may make the argument for homogeneity on the grounds that the range of pupil ability is decreased and the total group is more manageable in its segregated state.

The issue of heterogeneous or homogeneous grouping presents two different ways of thinking about how students are arranged for learning. In extreme situations, the disputes on this subject are fierce.

The subject speciality of a teacher may indicate a particular thinking emphasis or suggest potential competition between types of thinking in a faculty. Subjects in the curriculum may be symbolic and idealized, mathematic and scientific, social and problematic, cultural and utopian, or normative and aesthetic (3). A teacher's speciality may indicate his underlying preferences and values. In many school systems art and social science teachers seem to have fundamentally different attitudes about education and educational issues than do mathematics and Latin teachers; these differences may represent different ways of thinking about common problems.

Perhaps the most obvious examples of possible differences in thinking are the actual techniques used to reach particular teaching goals.

Many teachers use a combination of lecture and student recitation to promote learning of subject matter. The choice of these methods may reveal certain values in the teacher. First, there is a body of information which is to be learned. The information is given to the student in a tightly wrapped package; the student returns the package by reversing the lecture process; the information which is considered important exists apart from the student; and there are prescribed answers to given questions. The lecture-recitation technique also reveals the teacher's values or beliefs about the reliance of words and speaking to transmit learning. His key to learning is stimulus and response.

Other teachers rely primarily on demonstrations and student projects as the primary vehicles for learning. These methods may also say something about the teacher's values and ultimate goals. Learning is seen as part of the child rather than being information and the method by which it is transmitted, demonstrations are used to promote questions by the child and problems which lead into investigation, and projects allow the child to actually do something with a problem. The doing will increase personal awareness and allow the student to find his own meaning. These methods are based on the assumption that each person must experience and interpret something if it is to be real, a far different view of the type of thinking necessary for learning than the stimulus-response orientation. The teacher feels that other senses besides speaking must be brought into play to reach the goal of actual learning.

Discussion of possible differences in thinking would be incomplete without the topic of discipline. The controversy surrounding student control is commonly acknowledged and seems to be growing as an issue.

A classroom, school, or society must have certain regulating mechanisms in order to carry out a specified function. Assuming a minimum level of control is necessary in all educational situations, the question of discipline is not whether students are controlled but *how* control is exercised (4). A classroom must have a minimum level of ordered conduct to educate students, but there seems to be a difference between those teachers who justify control by outside authority and those who see control as intrinsic to the student.

Many teachers rely on authority outside the child to justify discipline. Rules are laid down by the teacher, the principal, the school system, the board of education and, ultimately, the electorate; in all cases, the conceptions of right-wrong and student control are predetermined. The child who fails to conform to the rules from "above" is disciplined by the superordinate authorities and faces a hierarchy of penalties, ranging from a mild rebuke to suspension or expulsion. The penalties, like the rules and the authority for control, are determined above the student's influence.

A second view of discipline puts the burden of maintaining control on the student. The vast majority of classroom rules rely on student self-discipline. Rules that must be administered from above for

survival of the school system are explained to the students and unacceptable behavior is spelled out so that the potential offender can
see the consequences before committing a violation. Teachers favor-
ing internal student control would put few external rules in the
"critical for system survival" category. The pupils have to consider
the moral dimension of unacceptable behavior by making the very
rules which govern and order them; the classroom is seen as a minia-
ture society of human relations where control is effected by personal
and social group norms.

The two approaches to discipline have caused violent clashes
of values among teachers. Some of them see student self-government
as an open invitation to anarchy while others see total control by external rules as a form of totalitarianism which supports authoritarian
personalities. The specific issue reflects fundamental preferences and
biases in the practitioner's thinking.

A final example of potential differences in thinking about the
teaching function is the question of student evaluation. A judgment
of teaching accomplishments depends on whether certain educational
purposes have been achieved. The different types of thinking about
student evaluation are shown by the purposes established by each
teacher and the way he analyzes them.

A teacher's particular purpose may be to transfer a body of information to the student, to train an immature mind, to develop the
ability to solve personal problems, or to awaken a sense of moral-
ity (5). Each objective has a different set of criteria against which
it can be evaluated. For example, if the transfer of information is
valued, the goal can be measured directly by the student's ability to
recall. Training the student's mind to think correctly can be tested
by clarity of expression or ability to interpret complicated mathematical and verbal problems. However, if the teacher's purpose is to
develop a student's ability to solve personal problems or to increase
moral commitment, the evaluation becomes complicated.

Both transfer of information and training of the immature mind
imply an outside standard of judging. The teacher can test the extent
of transfer, and can set the criteria to judge when a student's mind
"matures." In both cases, learning is evaluated on the student's demonstrated product.

The ability to solve individual problems or to act morally implies
a personalized, student-oriented judgment. When the purpose is to
develop a student's thought process rather than his thinking outcome,
evaluation becomes subjective and individualistic. The teacher cannot look inside a person to objectively assess new insights, commit-

ments, or growth in resolving difficulties; evaluation must be more subjective.

Each of the purposes and means by which teachers carry out their functions in the schools may represent a value framework and a form of thinking about practical problems.

The administrative function

The administrative function in education may also represent many different forms of thinking. These could be reflected in specific issues over school buildings, schedules, staff relationships, and other functions.

Many differences in administrative thinking may be seen in the school plant. Even the architecture might give clues to the values contained in administrative decisions. Some schools imitate office buildings, with light and air carefully controlled, and a design that stresses simplicity and functional aspects. The plant conveys a sense of efficiency, systematization, and rationality.

Other school plants lean the other way. The buildings look like physical monuments to some historical age or set of values. Huge Doric columns may suggest ancient Greece; massive walls, vaulted towers, and flying buttresses may place the building in a medieval period. This type of building could have the conscious purpose of conveying a particular mood.

Behind these particular architectural designs (and behind many others) may be values and preferences which express different kinds of thinking.

We might detect thinking differences by observing the physical interior of buildings. Some administrators desire movable walls and other features that permit altering the school's interior; other administrators prefer the fixed interior pattern. Some buildings are painted in bright, varied colors; others are cast in muted, constant color. These things suggest differences in thinking. If a curriculum is to be constant and unchanging why would a building need internal flexibility? If learning is a "serious" business why would attempts to improve the aesthetic qualities of the school be necessary?

An administrator may reveal a particular way of thinking when describing his relations with other personnel in the school system. The administrator may describe his relationship as "manager," as a "line" officer ("commander" if he is chief school officer), as a "human relations" expert, or as a "coordinator." Each label may connote different feelings about people and the school organization.

The "manager" or "line" officer could see himself and others as cogs in the wheel which represents the total school system, and could identify each person as a constant who carries out a particular educative function. The impersonality which seems to underlie this type of thinking may dictate that students, teachers, and possible administrators act as interchangeable, replaceable parts.

The "human relations" administrator is more likely to view others in the school system as unique personalities. In fact, his view of the total organization may not extend beyond his particular school or department.

The "coordinator" may also think in personalized terms but his view of the organization may be more expanded than just "human relations." This administrator may see others as groups and his role as walking the tightrope between organizational and personal needs.

Educational philosophies

If educational values and practices can be assumed to differentiate, in gross fashion, various thought processes, the directed thinking form can be compared to others. The particular meaning of a process stressing rationality, objectivity, and systematic application can be further clarified by identifying similarities to and differences from other forms of thinking; most present-day forms of educational thinking can be identified by a historical perspective which is exemplified in certain individuals or time periods. Directed thinking represents a composite of a number of historically-documented thought processes.

When a particular form of thinking becomes formalized or well-known it becomes a philosophy (6). For the sake of simple comparison, current educational forms of thinking can be distinguished by the way two fundamental questions are answered:

1. Is reality seen as something absolute or relative?
2. Does a person know what is real by direct experience and observation or by some other method?

Through analysis of the answers given to these two questions by other types of thinking, their relationships to the directed-thinking process can be determined.

At least seven philosophical bases can be identified in present educational thought. Each philosophy can be identified with a par-

ticular individual who, in rough fashion, represents a specific thinking form. Plato, Aristotle, St. Augustine, Francis Bacon, Charles
Darwin, John Dewey, and Jean-Paul Sartre each represent different
views of what is real and how people know. Portions of at least four
philosophies are an intregal part of the directed thinking process.

Platonism

Many philosophies have considered reality as absolute. Plato
was an early proponent of absolute truth, describing truth in terms
of certain universal, abstract ideals (7). The reality of these ideals
were eternal facts, immutable and unchanging.

Plato felt that truth was known through abstract reasoning and
intellect. To him, intellectual thinking was divorced from the human
senses; a person did not know reality by seeing, hearing, touching,
feeling, or tasting, but experienced the ultimate realities by abstract
thinking. Plato described a pyramid of knowing made of three hierarchical levels. The lower two levels, imagination and sense perception, could give opinion, but only the highest level of abstract thinking
could find fact. The pyramid of knowing is illustrated in figure 3.

Figure 3   Plato's Pyramid of Knowing

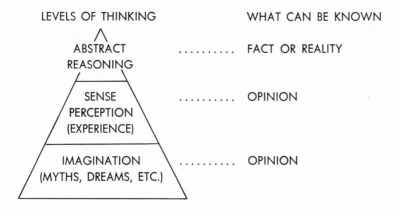

An example of Plato's type of knowing may be demonstrated with the concept of a circle. A person may see (or sense) many circles, but none of these experiences can give the true meaning of circularity. The perfect circle (an abstract concept *above* what can be experienced) exists only in the mind.

The belief that reality is made up of universal facts which was found in the Platonic age over two thousand years ago, can also be found in education today. There are citizens who demand that schools teach the "essentials" or give their children the "real" truths of learning; idealism similar to that esteemed by Plato is a value held by many people in present day society (8).

Certain proponents of current education emphasize the training of the mind through a study of the Great Books. This is a Platonic idea. These people see the key to knowing as a series of purely intellectual exercises to develop the capacity for abstract reasoning.

The Platonic approach has little similarity to directed thinking. Directed thinking does not assume idealized or absolute truths. Reality is not found solely through abstract reasoning. Directed thinking does stress use of the intellect, but not the intellect divorced from the senses; intellectualization is carried on through information derived by the senses.

Aristotelianism

A modification of Plato's thinking was presented by Aristotle (9). Aristotle rejected many of Plato's philosophical assumptions but agreed that reality consisted of general truths which were absolute. He differed from Plato's approach to knowing through abstract reasoning by believing that the search for universal facts begins in the senses. Again using the example of a circle, according to Aristotle a thinker justifies the universal reality of circularity by abstracting the *essence* of a circle from the experience of seeing many actual circles. Aristotle felt that a formalized process of logic would abstract reality from sensory experience. In present-day education the demand to train students' minds by formal logic is still heard, and thinking is perceived by many people as a process of dealing with "givens" and deriving logical "proofs".

The Aristotelian of today is revealed in the following conversation:

Aristotelian: "Given X=Y, and Y=Z, then X must equal Z."
Listener: "Yes, but where did X, Y, and Z come from?"
Aristotelian: "That question is meaningless because X, Y, and Z are given."

The social world has shown that it is possible to be logically consistent in thinking, yet far removed from reality.

Directed thinking derived two major ideas from the Aristotelian form of thinking. They are the reliance on a person's senses to guide thinking, although directed thought does not hope to find universal facts, and the *deductive* approach to reasoning. Although sharing the idea of deduction, Aristotelian logic differs from directed thinking by the assumption of previously known or accepted facts (the assumed X, Y, and Z). Because facts are given, the Aristotelian thinker focuses on the process of logic in itself. People who use directed thinking do not assume "givens" to which the deductive process is applied: consequently, they can use deduction to discover new facts.

Directed thinking borrowed the logical consistency necessary in deductive thinking. The logic of Aristotle pointed out the critical necessity of distinguishing consistently between a general explanation and a specific fact. Consistency is supported when an explanation is begun with an "if" or stated with a questioning inflection, and when the conclusion that follows is a logical consequence of the explanation. This is the "if-then" sequence. For example, an educator making the statement "all Irish children are lazy" would have to convert the explanation to "*if* all Irish children are lazy *then* Alice McCall must be lazy" (assuming Alice was an Irish child). The importance of logical links between a general explanation and a specific fact can be tested. If Alice McCall proves not to be lazy, then the explanation about all Irish children is also questionable.

Augustinism

Another major thinking movement dealing with questions of what is real and how we know is identified with St. Augustine and the early Christians (10). Reality was designated by the authority of God or his chosen interpretors. The facts about God were absolute and unchanging and many existed beyond human understanding.

The ultimate means of "knowing" was through faith. St. Augustine's pyramid of knowing was a translation of Plato's diagram with faith placed in the highest category. Figure 4 shows St. Augustine's pyramid.

Figure 4   St. Augustine's Pyramid of Knowing

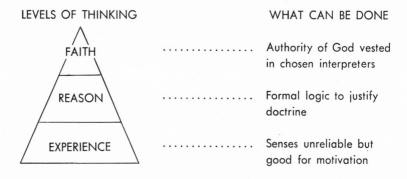

In Augustinian thinking, faith was seen as the most reliable method of knowing, because an all-perfect God could not deceive his children ("can neither deceive nor be deceived") and therefore faith must be truth. The abstract reasoning of formal logic was used to justify the faith ("Mind superior to matter," Rom. 7:22). The senses were seen as unreliable means of thinking because the physical world presents an imperfect representation of God's universe.

The influence of religion in education today is extensive, an obvious example being the parochial school system. In addition, many aspects of public education are affected by the St. Augustinian orientation to reality and knowing. Many times educational decisions are explained in terms of "you will have to take my (our) word for it," or "just have faith in me (us)." Although the religious aspect is missing, the rationale is a direct copy of what was reality to the chosen interpreters of early Christianity.

The directed thinker has few things in common with the Augustinian thought process. The absolute truth of God is not assumed by the directed-thinking process and faith is not a part of it.

Historically the religious emphasis associated with St. Augustine's thinking was followed by a reaction, largely against the chosen interpreters of God's word; those claiming divine interpretation were challenged by others who looked to human interpretation of the Word. Thinking then shifted to reliance on man as a thinker rather than man as a divine interpreter. By the 16th century the reliance on man as knower had led to a questioning of the idea that reality is absolute. Faith, ideals, and formal truths were swept aside by the scientific or liberal movement.

Empiricism

Two men associated with the scientific movement at different times were Bacon and Darwin (11, 12). In their thinking forms both men were empiricists; they treated as fact only those phenomena which were directly observable. However, these philosophers represent two different methods of using observation and developed somewhat different thinking processes. Francis Bacon is identified closely with the *inductive* approach to reasoning. The inductive thinker begins with direct observation of many individual facts or pieces of evidence, and then, after being immersed in the factual world long enough to observe a series or variety of situations, he arrives at general conclusions about reality. The knowing process begins with a wide, undifferentiated search for facts. Based on the information gathered, generalizations are made.

Directed-thinking educators use induction in two phases of the decision-making process. Before an educational issue is clarified in a particular area the educator is constantly searching for facts, not in terms of a concrete purpose (*e.g.* to make a decision about a problem) but to insure his generalized awareness of the educational environment. Then after the decision-making process actually produces a decision the educator analyzes his conclusion inductively. The decision is compared with environmental realities and with the original premises which the educator held at the problem-definition stage.

Directed thinking differs from the Baconian approach in its use of predictions or guesses about the outcome that are incorporated in the decision-making process. The use of predictions or *hypotheses* also differentiates Charles Darwin from Bacon. Darwin represents the evolution of the scientific movement from strict induction at its beginning to use of the hypothesis at its high point. Once a problem is defined in Darwinian thinking, a hypothesis about possible resolution or plausible explanation is set. This prediction guides the actual process of gathering and analyzing selected information and providing criteria by which to make a decision, rather than relying on personal inferences to somehow arrive at generalizations from interpreted facts.

The total scientific movement also developed methodological skills in collecting and analyzing information. Objectivity and rationality were specified as guides to decision-making, truth was tentative and people knew only what they could experience. The facts were based on the findings of empirical science. This meant reality was tentative, and it could change when the facts of observed situations changed. Knowledge was gained through the senses and they were directed by methodological guidelines.

Directed thinking shares the views of reality and knowing with the scientific movement. However, it differs in its degree of formalization and reliance on strict methodological procedures. Unfortunately, in the heyday of empiricism and scientism (16-18th century), an extreme desire to be objective created an unbending thought process which caused some scientific thinkers to attempt a purge of *all* human influence. This portion of the scientific movement focused on the physical sciences where workers applied strict controls and considered facts as constants. However, directed thinking borrowed heavily from the scientific method. Some of the rules of the scientific method which it retained include:

1. A fact must be directly observable.
2. Any explanation must be transformed into a factual prediction.
3. A prediction must be testable; there must be the possibility of showing the prediction to be implausible.

These rules were applied to thinking to insure a degree of uniformity in the process; if the scientific method was followed another thinker should be able to duplicate the process and find the same results. Consider Alice McCall once more. If the educator wants to test her "laziness," all criteria for being lazy must be directly observable. There must also be a prediction which includes the possibility of being wrong; the prediction can only be shown true if Alice actually meets the criteria that define laziness.

Directed thinking modified the steps of the scientific method to guide everyday decision-making. The concept of testability remains. Facts must be experienced by a person and cannot be merely assumed to exist. Predictions must be factual. The educator who says, "I'll bet the new children from the ghetto are dirty" has not made a factual prediction. The prediction also violates directed thinking because in its present state it cannot be demonstrated to be tenable or untenable.

Education has felt a resurgence of the desire for objectivity in the current "scientific movement" which is exemplified by the space race. Certain people see importance only in the physical world; the world of controllable, constant information. These people emphasize the physical sciences and mathematics and do not consider the "subjective" world of the social sciences constant enough to warrant serious attention. The directed thinker would disagree with this viewpoint.

Deweyism

A fifth form of thinking was the problem-solving approach of Dewey (13). He looked upon the scientific method, an outgrowth and synthesis of Aristotle, Darwin, and Bacon, as an integral part of all thinking, not just a way of testing physical facts, and he adopted the scientific process to provide a simple step-by-step way of thinking. Reality was experience that was found through an active use of a person's senses; knowing was the result of the senses being applied in a systematic, rational process of solving personal problems.

Dewey believed that education was a social function and that the institutions of education must serve a societal end. An educational thinker cannot be content with findings which are only descriptions of factual results; he must also predict the social consequences of his findings. Results or conclusions must be presented in terms of social use.

Directed thinking is an outgrowth of John Dewey's socially-oriented approach, and it too demands a social awareness. There are few, if any, problems in education which lack social implications. Even to resolve questions of building construction we must consider the community, the physical factors which facilitate or deter learning, and many other social concerns. The strict empiricist balks at the part of directed thinking concerned with social use. For him, thinking cannot go farther than an actual description of what is found, but the directed thinker is forced from the purely objective stance by the social nature of education.

Existentialism

A final form of thinking is represented by Jean-Paul Sartre (14). Actually, Sartre represents no philosophic system or doctrinaire thinking-form but rather a personal state of mind. His philosophy, existentialism, is based on the idea that each man is free to define his own nature; man is neither rational (Platonic), spiritual (Augustinian), nor a social product (Deweyan). Reality is always subjective and is dependent on the free choice of the thinker. Consequently, knowing does not come from past experience or from reason; a person "knows" through introspection and intuition arising from the personal experiencing of an instant.

Some educators follow Sartre by denying all efforts to know or state reality except as a personal phenomenon. Another group in this category are the alienated youths who attempt to drop out of society and live by a "do your own thing" philosophy. Directed thinking is not similar to existentialism for two major reasons. First, it uses standards or criteria that exist outside a person and that have value in guiding decision-making; knowing is not just an intuitive, introspective gesture. Second, directed thinking assumes that there is some continuity or regularity in reality which allows prediction of the future.

Directed thinking: a composite process

The directed-thinking process represents a composite of a number of philosophical premises. Figure 5 outlines specific steps in decision-making, which are derived from describing a problem, testing an argument, and interpreting results, and shows philosophers or philosophical movements that contributed to directed thinking.

The philosophical roots of directed thought represent a variety of different views about thinking. From them a practical process emerges for making educational decisions. Directed thinking represents both a controlled method for making practical decisions and a firm philosophical foundation for our thought.

Figure 5   Philosophical Bases of Directed Thinking

	Decision-Making	Major Contributor
Stages	Steps	
Describing problem	awareness of environment	Bacon
	problem definition	Aristotle
	hypothesis setting	Darwin
	information collection	scientific
Testing	information analysis	movement
Argument	making decision	Darwin
		Dewey
Interpreting Results	interpret to original problem	Bacon
	interpret for social use	Dewey

Questions

1. What are Plato's views of reality and knowing?
2. How does Aristotle differ from Plato's description of knowing?
3. What is the relationship of faith to reality and knowing according to St. Augustine?
4. What is the essential difference between the methods of thinking demonstrated by Bacon and Darwin?
5. What was Dewey's contribution to the scientific method?
6. What is social use?
7. Why can an existentialist never engage in directed thinking?
8. What specific contribution(s) did Bacon, Aristotle, Darwin, and Dewey make to the directed thinking process?

4

The Political Side
of Directed Thinking

Directed thinking is only one of the competing forms of educational thought. Some of our school systems have become the arena for the various types of thinking. People demand that educators return to the fundamentals of learning with the same fervor that Plato displayed when he stated the existence of universal ideals, and others argue for a curriculum of scientific and physical facts as though they were dyed-in-the-wool empiricists of the late 16th century. Meanwhile the existential citizen insists that the public schools be abandoned because they are totally irrelevant.

These varying philosophies demonstrate that the educational environment is a political world. The political nature of education is caused by the competing forms of thinking, of general societal characteristics, and of fundamental value questions which we have discussed in earlier chapters; the idealist, essentialist, and existentialist compete to promote their particular views of reality. The uncertainty, complexity, immediacy, and competition in education generate a hectic, explosive atmosphere. Education mirrors society; the fundamental questions of religion, race, ethics, and politics have no pat answers.

Western societies are generally based on a democratic political orientation. The democratic ideal emphasizes the practical aspects of debate, disagreement, and majority rule in making decisions; it discourages the political situation where final answers to societal questions are given "from above."

In a democratic climate the decision-making factors of personal influence, power, and the ability to sway the opinions of others become important. But unfortunately, the word "politics" causes an immediate negative reaction in some educators. To be accused of "playing politics" in education is an insult. Politics might suggest either smoke-filled backrooms and pot-bellied men with long cigars (1) or a corporate military-industrial complex manipulating values and desires by auto-suggestion, computers, and money.

There is growing recognition and acceptance, however, that education is political in most aspects. Politics is not an evil but a fact of educational life. Superintendents and board members who battle for a bond referendum know the political nature of education; the principal who tries to get additional resources for the local school recognizes the political bases of educational life; the teacher who works on a committee to develop school policy about student discipline has seen and used political influence. In this positive light, politics means actively promoting your ideas and values in a climate of competition, a type of political activity that is supported by the values of our democratic society and its educational institutions.

The decision to use directed thinking in practical situations may be highly political.

Directed thinking represents a constant, reliable way of analyzing a variety of problems. This very consistency may get the educator into trouble, for the systematic, objectively oriented thinker is in the minority. In some situations, the chances of making educational decisions objectively and surviving in the school system are very poor; schools are often run by subjective values. The directed thinker who suggests a systematic appraisal of present values may be an anathema.

The fact that the use of directed thinking may be a political decision does not imply that other forms of thinking are free from politics; the educator who chooses not to use directed thinking must accept some other type of thinking which also will have political overtones. When a person is committed to a particular value position, whether that of directed thinking, idealism, or strict empiricism, he will defend those values, and such a defense will mean political participation in the educational world.

Rationale for political competition

We have seen many of the specific reasons for political competition, but two underlying reasons which we have not yet discussed adequately are the fundamental issues facing current society and the problem of value translation.

Western society, and particularly the United States, is deep within a crisis period (2). Many people argue that current society is unique in the seriousness of its present issues. Of course, each generation feels that its own period in history is unique, but it does seem that current society *is* facing political, religious, sociological, and economic issues beyond the scope of any historical comparison. The past consequences of a wrong decision, for example, have never threatened complete destruction of a particular way of life. Societies have fallen because of the inability to resolve issues, but our present ability to destroy civilization adds a new dimension to current life. All of our societal problems are reflected in our educational system. Educators face demands to negate drugs and political erodings of society's fabric. The issue of church and state relations is intertwined in the question of public prayer in schools. The sociological implications of racial integration by bussing students and the economic issues of passing bond referendums in a "tight money" economy further emphasize the involvement of education in societal issues.

The second underlying reason that education is an arena of political competition is that varying specific translations can be made of the accepted abstract societal values. Most societies espouse a framework of abstract values which provide only the most general direction. For example, the United States makes four fundamental value assumptions which have direct impact on American education (3).

The first value is the right of all people to education; the rationale is that a democratic state cannot function without an educated citizenry. A related value is that each person should have the opportunity for the maximum education he can attain. A third value is that education provides a key to a better life; life is most meaningful and abundant (in all senses) when a person is fully educated. The final value basic to American education is control by the people; the vital decisions affecting public education must reflect the desires of the people.

But the translation of these abstract values can take many forms. The generalized societal values of Russia are remarkably similar to those of the United States; there are the same professed desires for democracy, protection of rights, and individual freedom. However, the practical application of these similar values differs radically in the two countries. The point is clear. Positive abstract national values can be translated into concrete forms that actually threaten the values they represent. The translation phenomenon also occurs when certain local communities within the United States make their own concrete interpretations of such general values as democracy, equality, and freedom.

In American life the local community has direct impact on the education system; school policy is directed by lay control through a local board of education (4). When policies are made, a specific local translation of values may provide the unwarranted aura of societal legitimacy to a particular community bias. Three examples in the United States demonstrate the problem.

The first example is that of autocratic control. Communities differ significantly in the distribution of political power among their people; in spite of the democratic ideal for political decision-making, all people do not exercise the same influence (5). Community issues are often decided by political leaders or influential citizens who exercise a disproportionate amount of power and who form the community political power structure. Some local communities have very rigid power structures which resemble pyramids, with a few political leaders controlling the decision-making on all community issues. In other communities there are many political leaders who compete in the exercise of power and influence.

Political leaders hold different educational beliefs, which usually can be determined by examining the community power structure they represent. Leaders of pyramid-type power structures are generally more closed in their beliefs about education than leaders of competitive power structures (6). The translation of values for education in a monolithic system can take extreme forms. The beliefs of community political leaders may dictate a certain type of educator in the school system. In pyramid communities the schools may be periodically purged of all "hippie, freak, subversive, briefcase-toting educrats." Directed thinking, which demands objective analysis rather than a particular political bent, may incur the wrath of influential community members.

The potential for misinterpreting religious values, our second example, remains strong in many local communities. Educators are constantly questioned about their attitudes regarding the Bible or public prayer in schools; these local challenges show that even the specific interpretation of the U.S. Supreme Court is not enough to halt value translation at the community level (7). An educator may make a directed-thinking judgment about a religious issue that supports a federal decision and contradicts the local translation, but such a judgment may cost him his job because of community reaction.

Probably no issue arena is more subjective, volatile, or potentially negative to directed thinkers than our third example, the translation of racial values. Community groups demand concrete commitments of educators on value translations. Sometimes demands are based on pure emotion and consciously deny factual information.

For many years the most overt example of subjective translation was the white, southern segregationist who demanded racial separation for any number of reasons (God's will, biological inferiority, etc.), but at present, the educator may also be attacked by subjective or rationalistic judgments from blacks (8). An argument that *only* black teachers must teach black studies programs is predicated on the "black experience." Attempts to explain the uniqueness of black experience run from skin pigmentation to psychological state of mind. If a directed-thinking educator points out that other races differ from white in skin color and other groups have been psychologically deprived, the charge of overt racism (if he happens to be white) or "Uncle Tom" (if he is black) is almost automatic.

The possible consequences of particular value translations *force* an active role in the political world upon educators, and especially upon research-minded educators who recognize that the social world is not composed of clear-cut right and wrong values.

It is easy for most educators to identify and shake their heads about the local community's translation of societal values and the resulting dangers to objective thinking, but the educational organization itself offers a constant challenge to the political survival of the directed thinker. It enforces a more subtle form of thinking control than that of the local community, but one that may be even more constricting.

School systems are divided into a series of superordinate-subordinate relationships for decision-making. Within the organization much problem solving is determined by rules and a hierarchical basis of graded authority (9). The normal flow of responsibility for decisions is from the board of education through the central office to the local school. Most educators, whether teachers, principals, or superintendents, can identify organizational positions above, below, and equal to theirs in authority.

In effect, the organizational position may replace any particular thinking process for determining the solutions to problems. The autonomy for individual thinking within an organizational structure may be very limited.

Beyond the formal organizational constraints the interpersonal relationships among educators play a big part in deciding the environment for thinking. There are philosophically liberal and conservative educators. Some educators rely on facts and some on subjective values to make decisions. The potential for negative reaction to directed thinking depends on the personalities of the people as they function in organizational relationships.

The situation where a superordinate may have negative control over a directed thinker is obvious. The superintendent who relies on the "tried and true" principles of good administration may conflict with the principal who wants to assess facts in the relative light of his particular situation.

Potential negative reactions from subordinates are also possible. A faculty used to a benevolent despot as a principal may not accept the local school administrator who does not claim to have all the answers and wants to use a directed-thinking approach.

Finally, the organization itself may consciously support discrepancies in the translation of values and the organizational practices may contradict a factual consideration of the educational purpose. For example, the specific type of pupil-assessment procedure used in the schools may violate the general value of continuous progress held by the particular school system.

Political strategies and tactics

Despite the foregoing deliberately bleak picture of negative reactions to directed thinking, political activity can overcome many such reactions and promote a positive climate for thinking. The educator must devise political strategies and tactics to protect his thinking from community and organizational attacks.

Like politics, the words "strategy" and "tactics" seem out of place in a discussion of education. These words seem more appropriate in military operations or labor and management bargaining. If the practicing educator feels more comfortable substituting such phrases as "long range planning" and "specific means of carrying out the plans," the meanings are generally synonymous.

When a directed thinker arrives at a judgment or decision he must set strategies or long range plans for its implementation (10). He may plan to change a particular situation or to maintain a current situation against attack. The directed thinker must analyze the educational situation in terms of implications for his judgment about an issue and then list the possible ways either to change or to maintain an environment. If change is needed he must list feasible alternate plans; if maintenance is crucial, he must list alternate defenses.

Once strategies are carefully laid out, concrete tactics or means of implementation must be specified. A tactic lists the "who, what, where, and how" of implementing a particular strategy (11). The importance of implementing strategies and using tactics in a political climate cannot be overemphasized. The directed thinker who is content only to make judgments in the rough-and-tumble educational world may not survive as an effective educator, for the environment, both inside and outside the school system, may either eliminate or isolate him.

The following example is a hypothetical situation in which a directed-thinking educator makes and implements her judgments in a political environment.

Mrs. Edith Jones is an experienced teacher at Rockdale High School. Rockdale is a politically active community and the school system reflects this activity on certain educational issues; because of the small-town atmosphere of the school and community most issues are handled in a highly personal manner.

Mrs. Jones engaged in directed thinking for some time but she also remained politically neutral. Consequently, she found many of her quiet judgments on issues totally disregarded. Over a period of time the frustration of being either alienated and ignored or patronized by others caused her to do some hard thinking on the basic question of whether it is possible to apply the principles of directed thinking to influence political decision-making.

Then three issues arose over which Edith Jones felt she must have some influence. The first issue was a question of changing the grading system for Rockdale. The second issue concerned the discipline case of Bill Brown, a Rockdale High School student, who allegedly ran an extortion racket on other students. The final issue involved Miss Wicket, a teacher for twenty years at Rockdale, who was to be transferred for incompetence.

Mrs. Jones thought about these issues in a directed manner, letting the systematic guidelines control her perceptions and personal feelings. She arrived at three conclusions.

1. The grading system was not consistent with program objectives of the Rockdale School system and was in need of change.

2. Bill Brown did not operate an extortion racket although he did have the reputation of being a troublemaker.

3. Thelma Wicket did not seem to meet legal or extra-legal definitions of incompetence. However, Mrs. Jones recognized she exercised less directed thinking in this issue because Thelma was a close friend.

Analysis of the current political situation

Edith Jones set down a list of people who had general influence which could affect educational decisions, dividing them between those who were members of the general community and those who were within the school system.

Those in the community who had influence were a lawyer who was also on the school board, a banker, officials at the teachers' union, a parent who "had the principal's ear," and members of a group called Citizens for Better Schools. In the system, the principal and four teachers of Rockdale High School determined most controversial school issues. The area superintendent and chief school officer also were influential.

Assessing these factors, Mrs. Jones divided her sources of influence in two ways, by their location and by their influence level (12). This division is shown in figure 6.

Figure 6

Influence Level

	Rockdale High School	System-wide
Community	Parent Citizens For Better Schools	Lawyer (School Board) Banker Teacher Union
School System	Principal 4 Teachers	Area Superintendent Chief School Officer

Location

After the initial classification of general influence, her second step was to match the sources of influence with the three issues (13). She did this by analyzing three things, the expected *effect* of an issue upon the source, the anticipated *involvement* of the source, and the expected *reaction* of the source. Edith knew that, usually, the greater the effect of an issue on a person the more direct his involvement. The expected reaction told her to whom she could look for support and from whom to expect opposition.

Edith decided to focus on the issue of grading change to test the directed-thinking application. For this purpose she further classified sources of influence as shown in figure 7.

Figure 7   Issue: Change in Grading Procedures

	Sources of Influence	Immediacy of Effect	Type of Involvement	Expected Reaction
School	Chief School Officer	G	D	N
	Area Superintendent	G	I	N
	Principal	S	I	?
	4 Teachers	S	?	?
Community	Lawyer (Board Member)	G	D	N
	Banker	G	?	?
	Parent	G	?	?
	Citizen Group	G	I	?
	Teacher Union	S	D	P

Key: *Effect* of issue on sources

S	= specific
G	= general
?	= cannot tell

Sources' expected *involvement*

D	= direct
I	= indirect
?	= cannot tell

Expected *reaction* to issue position

P	= positive
N	= negative
?	= cannot tell

The chart could be extended indefinitely for number of sources.

This issue seemed to be primarily a fight between the chief school officer, the lawyer, and the teachers' union. In this case, the lawyer was an outspoken board-member who wanted to be involved in the workings of education. The decision about this issue would be made outside Rockdale High School, so Edith Jones could expect her involvement to be indirect.

Mrs. Jones saw that her judgment for change was supported by the teachers' union but opposed by the lawyer board-member, the chief school officer, and the area superintendent. She did not know the probable reaction of the principal, but felt that he would be likely to side with the school organization and against her position if she attempted overt political influence.

Anticipated action

Edith Jones had analyzed the current political situation in regard to change in grading procedures and the potential or expected reactions of the sources of influence. Then came the fundamental personal judgment of whether or not to engage in overt political activity, really a decision as to personal visibility. A silent directed-thinking educator may continue without active opposition, but if Mrs. Jones felt she must make her position public she would then commit herself to the political arena. Direct and open opposition from other members of the school system would be a distinct possibility depending on the extent of her political action.

Assuming that Edith Jones chose to engage in political activity to further her directed-thinking judgment, the next question would be what type or types of action were most effective. She might actively attempt to influence her principal and the four influential Rockdale teachers to support the change in grading, but the issue was focussed at levels above the local school, and the support of local school personnel might gain no real political advantage, for political effectiveness is measured by actual impact on the decision of an issue (14). In this issue Edith Jones would probably have to work at the system-wide or general-public level. This might mean giving public speeches that would be picked up by the newspapers, appearing on TV panel shows, or participating actively in the teachers' union. The number and kind of local facilities that were actually available to Mrs. Jones for stimulating general interest could of course be factors that controlled her activities.

Types of influence resources

Influence resources can be described as any means available to defend or promote a point of view; they are the sources of political power that a person may call upon to influence others (15). They may take many forms. Educational resources can range from the power implicit in holding a formal position of authority to that gained by having psychological autonomy growing out of organizational and personality factors. The administrator's resource because of his official position in the school-system hierarchy is obvious, but it is not generally recognized that other groups or individuals in the organization have political resources which are potentially as powerful as hierarchial position. For example, the teacher in the self-contained classroom who can close the door on direct supervision has a powerful resource to control whether decisions are implemented.

The person who has interest in a single issue and can concentrate his efforts for influence upon it has more resources than a person who must spread the same amount of power over a number of issues. The educator whose predominant desire is to influence a particular issue may defeat a superior who must be concerned with many problems simultaneously.

A person who shows expertise also has a powerful political resource. The objective nature of a directed-thinking person may be a positive virtue in an educational situation where, for example, the value of efficiency and rationality may cause certain political elements to favor directed-thinking educators.

To demonstrate the use of these various kinds of resources, consider our hypothetical example of Mrs. Jones and the grading issue. She might be the Rockdale High School's representative to the union. She might also become so involved in the question of grading that she devoted a large percentage of her after-school time campaigning for support. Finally, Mrs. Jones might have served on a committee which made an intensive, year-long study of grading and grading procedures, in which case she would have a degree of expertise on the subject. The individual resources of position, time, and expertise thus could all be directed to the issue of grading. In addition, Mrs. Jones might seek and find other sources of positive group support, such as the Citizens for Better Schools.

The same method of using directed-thinking procedures to guide personal political activity could be followed for the issues of Bill Brown's discipline or the transfer of Miss Wicket. These are problems which originate in Rockdale High School, and Mrs. Jones probably would have a greater potential for direct influence and overt political activity in local school issues. The assessment of the current situation, choice of political action, type of action, and use of influence resources would be carried out in the same manner as in the grading issue.

This example is not the only possible way in which directed-thinking procedures could be applied to the political side of education. It does show, however, that practitioners can engage in the rough and tumble world of education in a systematic, rationally oriented manner.

Questions

1. Why is education not divorced from politics?
2. What is education's relation to society?
3. Why does political competition occur over most valued educational beliefs and ideals?
4. What are political power structures and how do they influence thinking?
5. Why must educators take a politically active role?
6. What is a political strategy and how does it differ from a tactic?
7. How can directed thinking be used to assess an on-going political situation?
8. How is the directed-thinking process applied to making political decisions?

Part Two
Scientific Inquiry

5

Scientific Inquiry — The Formal Process

Since the first chapter, this text has emphasized that the unifying bond between types of educators is a common thought process based on the concepts of objectivity, rationality, and systematic application. When the thinking is applied to daily decisions in the schools it is labelled directed thinking; it represents one end of the basic research-oriented thought-process continuum. The other end is labelled *scientific inquiry* and refers to the same fundamental thinking base when it is used by the researcher, rather than the practitioner. Strict scientific inquiry represents a stringent methodology with sets of highly specific procedures to guide thinking about research problems.

There is a wide range of activity between the two extremes of the continuum; applied research or action research may be less formal than pure scientific inquiry, and the farther that the educator departs from the strictest form, the more he becomes both researcher and practitioner — the "two-hat" concept we have discussed before. Figure 8 shows the relationship between research-oriented thinking and the educator's role.

Figure 8   Thinking and Role Relationships

60

As we have seen, in the 1970s the trend seems to be toward educators who mix the roles of researcher and practitioner in some combination. Likewise, the percentage of educators who blend directed thinking with the more formalized scientific inquiry will also grow in the next decade. These trends stress the need for increased awareness and understanding of educational research now and in the future.

Scientific inquiry, in the strict sense, attempts to approach what Charles Sanders Pierce calls the method of science.

It is necessary that a method should be found by which our beliefs may be determined by nothing human, but by some external permanency— *by something upon which our thinking has no effect* [italics added]. . . . The method must be such that the ultimate conclusion of every man shall be the same. Such is the method of science. Its fundamental hypothesis is this: There are real things, whose characters are entirely independent of our opinions about them (1).

This description implies the extreme interpretation of rationality, objectivity, and systematic application in thinking; the process or method of thinking is *entirely* divorced from the person. Reality exists in the method or guidelines that control thought, not in the individual thinker. This process differs from directed thinking which assumes, realistically, some personalization in the process of making educational decisions. However, we can see that all types of research-oriented thinking emphasize process over person in making judgments; differences between them lie in the *extent of modification* of the literal definition of method.

In many ways, strict scientific inquiry traces its historical roots to the scientific movement of the 16-18th century, and the philosophers identified with this period, Bacon, Darwin, and others, are the forerunners of present-day scientific inquiry. The concepts of induction, hypothesis, and deduction which characterize directed thinking also underlie scientific inquiry. Part II of this book outlines how the scientific-inquiry process is applied by the educational researcher.

Research in the various sciences

Along the continuum of research-oriented thinking there are a number of schools of inquiry that are called the sciences and that represent different contexts in which scientific inquiry is utilized. The contexts are distinguished by the *type* of research problem investigated and, to some degree, by the application of methodological guidelines which are followed to analyze the problem.

The most fundamental distinction between sciences is whether scientific inquiry is applied to a particular knowledge framework or to a combination of knowledge. Sciences with a particular focus — those such as physics, economics, and psychology — center their scientific inquiry on specialized areas of thinking. Others apply specific knowledge from the various specialized sciences to a complex social situation, forming a composite science by the interaction of the specific contexts. Education is one such combined science, for the educator must consider problems which involve psychology, biology, sociology, and politics. Figure 9 presents a schematic illustration of the relationship between scientific inquiry and the various sciences.

Figure 9   "Sciences": Contexts for Research Thinking

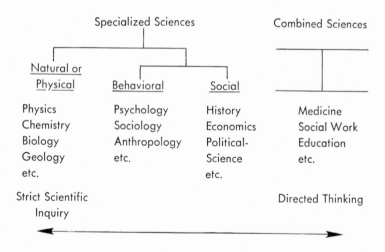

Specialized sciences

The specialized sciences are often divided into two sections; the physical or natural sciences and the social sciences (2). As the names imply, the physical or natural sciences deal with non-social problems while the social sciences are oriented to the study of human behavior and social organization (3). The physiological study of man in biology is considered a natural science but the study of man's behavior is carried out in the realms of the various social sciences.

If natural, social-behavioral, and combined sciences are classified as three distinct forms, it is logical that the basic thought processes of research must differ somewhat in their application to each one. The type of problem involved determines how rigidly the process of research thinking may be applied.

For example, in the natural sciences physics is concerned with molecules, atoms, and elements, which are relatively constant factors. When the physicist describes a situation he can state with certainty that the molecular structure of so-and-so is such-and-such, and he can collect information to support a prediction in an artificially controlled environment (4). The laboratory situation can physically impose or remove certain factors which may affect a problem. The researcher may test and interpret results with exact measures.

The natural sciences enjoy the highest degree of preciseness and certainty in the factors that make up a thinking situation (5). The thinker has confidence that a certain type of seed will be the same as other seeds of the same variety, a rock with certain characteristics will be the same as other rocks with the same characteristics, and this assumption of sameness is also true for blood cells, molecules, and chemicals. The researcher can apply the process of scientific inquiry very rigidly in the natural sciences, a "tightness" that affects the framework, process, and product of his thinking. He can be confident about many of the assumptions necessary for strict application of the basic thinking process.

Some of the assumptions of scientific inquiry when carried out in the natural sciences are:

1. Many of the factors being studied or used to define the problems will remain constant.

2. The methods of collecting information, the number of possible solutions, and the types of interpretation of results are limited.

3. Conclusions can be generalized and the process of thinking to reach particular results replicated.

Combined sciences

When we move on to study social problems, however, we cannot meet these assumptions; the predictability of human behavior is not the same as that of molecules. A researcher may study a rock and be able to predict things about a similar rock with a high degree of confidence, but another researcher who is studying a social situation can not have a similar confidence in human sameness. If anything, it is human *difference* which must be assumed and accounted for in the thought process.

Scientific inquiry in the social and behavioral sciences must explain the lack of sameness in the factors being studied. The thinker makes statements describing a situation, testing an argument, or interpreting results but he has a greater recognition and expectation of being wrong; scientific inquiry in the social or behavioral sciences *never* assumes sameness to the degree found in the natural sciences. This, of course, affects the application of the thinking process to social situations. Differences among people and social organizations must be identified, but social situations cannot be controlled like a physical-science experiment. Not all alternatives can be known or all information be collected. As a result, widely generalized conclusions are not possible; a political researcher would never state that "all politicians act like Mayor Smith."

Scientific inquiry, however, can be used in the combined sciences, although as we have seen, the complex, interacting nature of a combined science makes such use especially difficult. We are here particularly interested in applying the process of scientific inquiry to the combined science of education, which embodies a number of social and natural sciences. Educational problems involve the biological concerns of human health and intelligence, physical factors such as light and heat that affect an educational environment, social and economic differences in children, and political factors.

Beyond the complications of applying the scientific method in education is the further complication of the educational thinker himself. No person can ever be completely divorced from his personal preferences or biases; even the decision to engage in research or controlled thinking is the result of a value judgment. The tendency for personal values to enter thinking increases as the problem under consideration directly affects the thinker. We can see why research in education, a field rife with personal considerations and direct effect on an individual's life, may contain more bias than research in other sciences.

The educational researcher may also be impeded by the possible contradictions between the knowledge derived from doing research and the human values of the people involved in the research. For example, studying the extent to which people will comply with external authority may cause the subjects mental anguish and distress.

How does the researcher balance the potential detriment in procedures against positive outcome in results?

Search and research

Before discussing the application of scientific inquiry in a formalized research process, we must make the distinction between search and research.

The search process is an intregal part of the educator's thinking, whether he be practitioner or researcher. Before a problem or a specific need is defined, a person is in a state of general awareness of his environment. While in the environment, the person is struck with some indeterminate doubt, perplexity, or barrier, which must then be defined, and he struggles to grasp the problem or need which is causing him emotional disturbance.

When the thinker identifies the need to be fulfilled or the problem to be resolved he has moved from the process of search to one of research. The transition can be made by scanning his own experiences, by some intuitive guess, or possibly by an inventive leap of the mind. The crucial distinction is that the transition must actually be made before thinking can become a research-oriented process.

However, a directed-thinking educator or one engaged in scientific inquiry has one basic characteristic which can aid him in the *search* process. The *inductive process,* identified with Francis Bacon, guides a person's general awareness of his environment. Essentially this means that a person thus guided relies on fact-gathering rather than opinion even when a specific need or problem has not yet been identified; the research-oriented person is basically a rational, objective being even before engaging in specific decision-making or research.

The process of scientific inquiry in formal research

The process of formal research can be thought of as three interrelated stages or phases which must be considered by the educational researcher. They are shown in figure 10.

Figure 10   The Formal Research Process

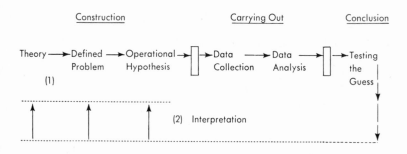

(1) Build a logically consistent bridge.

(2) Interpret conclusion in terms of hypothesis, then of problem, then of theory.

Notice that the process of formal research is *cyclical* rather than a straight line. The construction, carrying out, and conclusion stages of research are connected so that each is dependent on the preceeding and following phases. Because in a book we must follow a chapter organization in describing the formal research process, we may give the false impression that one phase of a specific research project can be considered in isolation, when in fact the various phases are totally meshed together. A researcher cannot discuss theoretical explanations without considering the testing of hypotheses. This in turn leads to questions about the specific operations used to carry out the formal research.

To change our simile, the formal-research process is like a structure made of a child's building blocks. The structure may be a skyscraper or a castle when all the blocks are considered together; pull one block out to consider it individually and the structure becomes a jumble. The educational researcher who only considers one aspect of the total process in formal research also runs the risk of intellectual jumble.

This is exactly the danger to the practitioner who must rely on reading only the results of a formal research report. The amount of confidence that a practicing educator can put in research conclusions depends upon how effectively the research was carried out, which in turn depends upon how well the questions of the construction phase were answered. The number of school systems who have made costly decisions based solely on the conclusions of formal research is staggering. How many innovations which were tested and gained optimistic conclusions are now gathering dust in school closets and storage rooms? These financial tragedies are largely the result of considering one aspect of formal research divorced from the total process.

The practitioner must keep in mind the total research process as he reads about the specific research operations. Direct questions, such as what statistics are used to study relationships or whether random sampling is to be used, have meaning only when they are asked in relation to the general process.

Construction phase

The construction phase may be the most important stage of formal research, for the ultimate purpose of all formal research is to build explanatory theory — explanations based on empirical testing of ideas by specified research methods. When a practicing educator asks why waste time with formal research, the best answer a researcher can give is that research builds tested explanations about practical problems. Unfortunately, the good researcher's description of what formal research should do is not always the same as what is found under the label of "formal research" in educational literature.

Construction of formal research involves three specific operations: defining a particular problem from a general explanation, setting the problem in the form of a prediction, and describing how the specific hypothesis is to be tested empirically. One operation builds from the other to form the construction phase. The reader should beware of reports that slight this phase.

Carrying-out phase

The carrying-out phase is determined by the construction phase and has as its primary purpose the analysis of the prediction or hypothesis made about the research question. Carrying out formal research involves selecting a research design that will collect the desired information and analyze data.

Understandably, this is the phase which is least familiar to practicing educators. The carrying-out phase has many specific rules which must be followed in operations and the language used in it is technical and different from what is used in school systems. Every day the practitioner hears words such as theory, prediction, conclusion, or interpretation, but less often does he deal with terms like design, coefficient, stratification, or factor analysis.

Both the rules and language of the carrying-out phase remove it from the normal world of the practicing educator. But, as we will discuss in detail later, the carrying-out phase has two major parts, the collection of information and the analysis of it in order to analyze predictions. Practitioners do both these tasks in their daily problem-solving; the difference here as elsewhere is still a matter of degree.

Conclusion phase

The conclusion phase of formal research also involves two operations, testing the hypothesis and interpreting results. Both these judgments are made according to specified rules of research. The test of the prediction or hypothesis is specified in the construction phase before the research is carried out, and a standard is set by which the experimenter later can judge whether the prediction is acceptable or not. The interpretive judgment of results is more difficult. If a prediction is accepted as true the researcher must then derive a theoretical explanation from the findings. This process involves generalization and inference which is based on logical consistency in the research process. The strength of the results will depend in part on how well the research was carried out.

Again it is evident that the practitioner must be able to judge the effectiveness of formal research procedures in order to analyze the results. He will find that the generalist approach, which sees formal research as an extension of a normal process of thinking, helps re-emphasize the totality of the research cycle. This approach will also allow him to analyze and use formal research as a valuable source of additional information in solving practical problems.

An approach to formal research

Our discussion of formal research methodology will be based on two assumptions. First, scientific inquiry can be described as a formalized extension of the form of everyday directed thinking. The stages of scientific inquiry are the same ones that a person uses when he thinks in a directed manner. The difference between everyday thinking and formal procedure is in degree, not kind; the criteria for good formal research are similar to the rules which govern directed thinking. The difference is the close tolerance with which formal research procedures must meet stated criteria before being accepted as worthwhile.

The second assumption is that information oriented toward "using" rather than "doing" formal research is most valuable in this initial introduction to the subject. Educational research is such a complex topic that whole books have been written on the matter contained in each of the following chapters; our introduction must concentrate upon the initial, practical needs.

Questions

1. How does scientific inquiry differ from directed thinking?
2. What are the sciences and how is scientific inquiry affected by the sciences?
3. How is the thinker affected by the use of scientific inquiry in social research?
4. What distinguishes the process of search from research?
5. Why is the formal research process cyclical in nature?
6. What are the specific operations incorporated in each phase of the formal research process?

6

The Language
of Formal Research

Formal research is often difficult to follow because of the language it uses. Terms like variable, parametric, validity, and statistic can be explained in everyday words, but often this is not done in educational research. Unsureness over meaning widens the gap between formal research and the practitioner. The meanings of certain words are crucial to understand and distinguish good and bad formal research for practical use.

Like words of any other language, research words are used in certain contexts and have restrictions placed on their meanings. Most expressions have antonyms; there are dependent and independent variables, for example, or parametric and non-parametric statistics. A brief description of certain crucial words may help in interpreting specific aspects of the formal research process.

Variables

A variable is any symbol or thing that has a value assigned to it (1). For example, "achievement" is a variable. So is "age," "socioeconomic standing," "color of hair" and so forth. Most variables in formal research are given numbers to represent their values. "Achievement" may be represented by the quantified scores of one or more tests. "Little" participation may be assigned a numerical value and become a quantifiable variable.

Variables may be termed *dependent, independent,* or *control* (2).

Often people not used to research have trouble distinguishing between independent and dependent variables in a formal research problem. By concentrating on the *dependent variable* we find several ways to keep the two clear.

1. The dependent variable *depends* on influence from the independent variable.
2. The dependent variable may be *affected* by the changes in the independent variable.
3. The dependent variable may be observed for variation *caused* by the independent variable.

If we reverse our approach and think of the *independent variable* the distinction is still clear.

1. If the independent variable changes then some effect should be observed in the dependent variable.
2. A researcher who manipulates the independent variable will watch for change in the dependent variable.

An example from the educational world may illustrate the distinction. Most educators are concerned about student achievement; suppose a practitioner wanted to find out the effect of a method of teaching on achievement. Which variable "depends" on the other? Achievement, of course, is the dependent variable which may be "caused" by a certain teaching method.

This example leads us to another fact of educational research. There are very few situations where there is only one independent variable or possible cause of the dependent variable; similarly, it is difficult to point to a single effect or dependent variable. If student achievement is treated as the dependent variable there is obviously a whole host of independent variables besides the teaching method. The students' personality, attitude toward school, and intelligence; the school environment; and the class atmosphere are all independent variables which might affect student achievement.

Many of the education variables described as independent could also be dependent variables in different situations. For example, attitudes toward school or personality could be dependent and student achievement could be an independent variable. In many cases of social research there are several independent and dependent variables which should be considered.

The researcher must therefore make a fundamental choice; will he attempt to analyze the impact of a number of variables simultaneously or will he attempt to isolate and control a single independent and a single dependent variable for study? If he looks at the combined effect of a number of variables he is doing *multivariate analysis*. If he controls the effect of certain independent variables he has created *control* variables. Much of today's social research has control variables, independent variables, and several dependent variables (3). Education is a complex world and to study one-to-one relationships between an independent variable and a dependent variable creates an artificial, simplistic picture. Control variables are needed because many independent variables are almost impossible for the researcher to manipulate.

For example, it is difficult to manipulate race, sex, or aptitude. It is hard to measure intelligence, aspiration, or anxiety. It may be easier to control these variables by a number of statistical techniques which are available.

Statistics

The word statistics can be confusing because it has two meanings. Statistics refers to the techniques or *processes* used for gathering, describing, organizing, analyzing, and interpreting numbers. The word also is used to describe the *product* or the numerical information which has been collected. The person faced with the term should first determine if statistics is being considered as a process, a product, or both. Both meanings of course deal with numbers; statistics is a tool of measurement which handles numerical data in formal research (4).

Statistical processes and products can be divided into two basic categories: *descriptive* and *inferential*.

Descriptive and inferential statistics

Descriptive statistics deal with a *whole* category. It is merely a description, by numbers, of a particular group. This type of statistics describes the group being studied and never attempts to generalize findings or extend conclusions beyond the study. When Mrs. Brown gathers numerical information about her 6th grade class she is engaging in descriptive statistics; as long as she does *not* attempt to compare her class with others or draw similarities to 6th graders in general Mrs. Brown will continue to use statistics in a descriptive manner.

Inferential statistics deal with a *part*. The majority of educational research uses this form of statistics, for two major reasons. First, there is a natural tendency to want to go beyond pure description of events. When a teacher studies her class or a principal judges his school, a major question is, by what standard are the numerical results to be analyzed? Descriptive statistics make no comparisons beyond the case under study; their results are a compilation or reordering of the actual numerical findings. Inferential statistics, on the other hand, compare the numbers under study with some outside standard. The standard may be some other class, school, the "average" 6th grader, or the odds of finding the results of the studied group by pure chance. In effect, inferential statistics takes a specific group or category (a part of the whole) selected by chance and compares it with a general case or total category. Statistical results then *infer* from the comparison the degree of likeness or difference between the specific and the general case.

Inferential statistics are also popular in formal research because of the problems of information-gathering for certain educational issues. Many times it is not possible to use a total group to get information; imagine the time and cost involved if a researcher wanted to study the attitudes of all teachers in New York, or in the state of Kansas, or in a whole country. When it becomes physically impossible to describe all members of a group individually then a *representative* number is studied. The smaller number, which is assumed to represent the total group, is called a *sample*. An inferential statistic is a numerical measure based on a sample. An inferential statistic deals only with a sample rather than with the total group. There is always a chance that the sample does not exactly represent the whole; we must remember that all inferential statistics have the built-in chance of being wrong (5). This is called the *error factor*. A major purpose of some inferential statistics is to give the researcher an estimate of the probability that the sample studied and the total group or population are statistically the same. We can see the amount of inference a particular researcher is making by looking at the *level of statistical significance*. For example, we may read of statistics assessed at the ".05 level of significance." This simply means that the researcher is willing to accept the statistical probability of sameness at 95 out of 100 chances, realizing there are 5 risks in 100 of being wrong.

The statement of statistical significance sets a level at which the educational researcher is confident that the partial group being studied and the whole population are in the same probability area.

Another way of saying this is that the level of significance sets the amount of probable error which a researcher is willing to accept and still consider that he is dealing with statistical sameness.

Much of education research, however, looks for statistical difference rather than sameness. A teacher wants to find if a special type of student is different from the rest of the students. In this case, the researcher hopes the sample (special students) and the population (rest of students) have significantly different probabilities.

A practitioner reads of two groups of children who were compared on reading achievement and received a numerical value of 6.210 which indicates the extent of difference between the groups. The researcher writes that the numerical value was accepted as an indicator of statistical difference between the two groups at .05 level of significance (6). The .05 means that the probability of the two groups responding as they did and receiving a value of 6.210 through pure chance is only 5 chances or less in 100 according to a mathematical table which compared found values with expected values (7). The researcher acknowledges he still might be wrong but he's willing to "bet" on the 95 "for" probability to 5 "against" as the odds for a real difference between the children. Most formal research in education is based on the .05 (5/100) or .01 (1/100) levels of statistical significance (8).

Figure 11 shows the division of statistics into descriptive and inferential and the further subdivision of inferential into *parametric* and *non-parametric* categories.

Figure 11   **Statistics: Process and Product**

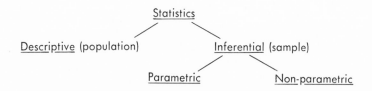

Parametric and non-parametric statistics

Both parametric and non-parametric statistics demand a *random sample*. Random sampling means that the choice of subjects for the sample which is to represent the total population is made with each subject having an equal chance to be chosen. The selection of one person is in no way dependent on the selection of any other. (The concept of randomization is further described in Chapter 9 on data collection.) All inferential statistics demand that the partial representation of the whole group be chosen by the luck of the draw.

Both parametric and non-parametric inferential statistic demand for study are independent of each other. The answer a person gives will not be influenced by another subject's score. Strict independence of scores is rarely achieved in social research but the lack of exactness is compensated for by probabilities of actual separation.

Parametric statistics differ from non-parametric statistics in the assumptions made about the total population from which the sample was selected. Parametric statistics assume a normal distribution. With a normally distributed population, a few people will score extremely high, a few extremely low, but most people will tend to cluster around the middle range of scores. Mathematicians as early as the 18th century worked out formulas based on probabilities and chance which demonstrated the idea of normal distribution in a total population (9). A complete normal distribution gives numerical information which plots on a curve resembling a bell. The bell-shaped curve is shown in Figure 12.

Figure 12

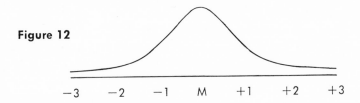

$-3 \quad -2 \quad -1 \quad M \quad +1 \quad +2 \quad +3$

Because of mathematical exactness, the spread of scores on each side of (M) are the same. The numerals 1, 2, and 3 on the diagram represent *standard deviations* measured from the center. (For further discussion of standard deviation, see chapter 10). Mathematically, a researcher knows that roughly two-thirds of all the people or subjects in a normally distributed population fall between plus and minus one standard deviation (10). In parametric statistics, it is assumed that in the sample which is drawn from a population the *spread of scores* will represent a normal distribution.

Another assumption of parametric statistics has to do with the type of *numerical value* used. All types of statistics deal with numbers but not all numbers are the same. If the numerical values used in statistics only rank people in relation to one another parametric statistics rarely can be used; the same is true when numbers are only used to classify. For example, blue eyes are labelled "1", brown eyes "2" and so forth. Parametric statistics can only be used when it is possible to apply the mathematical processes of addition and subtraction meaningfully. Numbers must be continuous and comparable on the same scale or at equal intervals.

The second form of inferential statistics are the non-parametric variety. There is considerable use of non-parametric statistics in education by researchers who wish to estimate and make predictions without making assumptions about the distributions of the population. One of the major differences between parametric and non-parametric statistics is the necessity when using the former to assume a normal distribution; when using non-parametric statistics we do not have to assume the normal distribution of the base population. Suppose a population of exceptional children (whether extremely bright or dull) was studied. The researcher would not expect to find the responses plotting in a bell-curve pattern; the curve would probably look like the leaning tower of Pisa. Because non-parametric statistics do not demand normality the responses of a drawn sample could still be compared to the population of exceptional children.

Often the type of numerical information a researcher gathers about educational subjects cannot meet parametric standards. Many topics, such as favorable attitudes about continuous progress, can only give the researcher a gross ranking of people. It may be that Teacher A likes continuous progress more than Teacher B but the researcher would be stretching the data to imply some sort of equal interval or exact scale for measuring "liking." The favorable attitude of Teacher A cannot be assumed to be exactly twice that of Teacher B; the gathered information is not that mathematically precise.

Non-parametric statistics are used when the distribution of the population is not known, when numerical information is used for ranking or labelling, or when less than 30 individuals are being studied (11).

The likenesses and differences of the two types of inferential statistics are caused largely by the mathematical rationale behind each technique. Parametric statistics are the "classical" and most widely used of the two methods. Non-parametric statistics are a modification to meet situations which fall outside the range of parametric assumptions.

Whether a particular parametric or non-parametric technique is the "best" statistic is a moot question. Parametric statistics are mathematically more powerful, in that greater confidence can be put in the results, but parametric statistics must also make more assumptions about the educational world being studied. On the other hand, non-parametric statistics are estimated to be only 90 per cent as efficient as parametric yet they make fewer assumptions about reality (12). The question of statistical use rests on the particular situation being studied. In questions about the situation studied, the information gathered, and general judgments about the appropriateness of statistics, the user of research can be a discriminating judge no matter how unfamiliar he is with the specific techniques involved.

Variance

A liberal definition of the word variance is the amount of difference between two or more things. The idea of difference is the key concept in most, if not all, formal research (13). However, there are several types of difference which may occur in formal research. Variance is the particular difference by which an individual's score varies from the average or mean score of a group. When the researcher knows the scores of individuals in relation to their average as a group he can get a measure of spread or total difference for the group. If certain individual scores are far from the group average there is large variance; if all individuals score close to the group average there is little variance. Figure 13 gives a picture of plotted individual scores in relation to their group mean and shows how a large variance differs from a small.

Figure 13

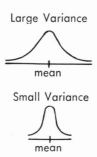

Large Variance

mean

Small Variance

mean

The reader can see that once the variance of a particular group is known, then this measure can be used as the basis for comparison against other groups. Most good formal research will compare groups on their average or middle scores *and* on their variances or extents of individual differences.

Variance may be found between two or more samples, between individuals within a sample, or between a sample and the total population. A researcher may want to see if there is any difference between the attitudes of selected social-studies and science teachers in a school system; he will analyze variance in each of the two samples. The same researcher may be interested in how closely the teachers agree in either the social-studies or science sample. This is a study of within variance. Finally, the researcher may want to infer the difference between the teachers of his selected sample and all social-studies teachers. This is a comparison for sample-population variance.

Variance, like most formal research analysis, is a statistical measure of numerical differences. Inferential statistics are concerned with two basic types of variance: *systematic variance* and *error variance.* Systematic variance is difference resulting from known or unknown variables that cause events to happen in a certain predictable way. The researcher hopes to identify and account for most of the variables in a research situation, but there is *always* some varying or difference caused by chance. This is called error variance. In the formal research analysis the difference which remains after the systematic variance is identified and accounted for is the error.

Reliability

Reliability is a term often associated with the results of research. Essentially, reliability means that the same results will be obtained whenever certain information is analyzed.

A reliable educator is someone who is dependable, consistent, or predictable; what he does today will be consistent with what he did yesterday and what he will do tomorrow. The same is true for the reliability of results in formal research. If results are reliable they are stable from occasion to occasion; they do not differ with the passage of time.

Notice that a reliable result is not necessarily a true or right answer. We all know someone who is quite consistent in doing the wrong thing time and time again. Some teachers must feel that certain students are obsessed or addicted to chewing gum in class; over and over Tom Jones comes to class with a wad of gum in his mouth; threats or pleas bring promises to stop gum-chewing which are always forgotten with each new class. Tom's gum-chewing and the teacher's response become a ritual. The predictability of Tom's action is high; he is a reliable person for doing the wrong thing.

We may find the term reliability associated with the gathering of research information as well as with the results. Reliability is often discussed in connection with test construction or observer training. The researcher wants to insure that a particular test or observer will be dependable in obtaining results. A reliable instrument should obtain essentially the same results each time the test is given; if it does, it has what is called "test-retest" reliability. A test should also be internally consistent; items in the first half, for example, should not have a disproportionate number of right answers. A check used to insure that there is no influencing pattern of item position in the test determines what is called "split-half" reliability.

Validity

Validity is a question about reality. It asks, "are we measuring what we think we are measuring?" Results can be reliable without being valid. A researcher who creates an instrument to measure participation may get the same responses to items again and again; the instrument is reliable but whether it is an actual measure of "participation" is another matter. Participation is a nebulous concept which is difficult to describe or measure. For example, attitudes toward participation may involve far different measures than actions indicating overt participatory behavior. Measuring what we think we are measuring is a complex task and validity may be a shifting thing (14).

We find that researchers attempt to establish validity in different ways. Content, construct, and predictive validity are three common types used in formal research.

Content validity is concerned with how representative the topic, the indicators, and the substance are that are used to measure an idea. In effect, the content itself (whatever the measure) becomes reality. Usually a panel of judges or experts state that the content of a measure represents reality; for example, if five professors of administration state that a particular test measures "administrative behavior" they have stated the validity of the content. Validity becomes a matter of logic; the danger is obvious that content validity produces a self-fulfilling prophesy. If the practitioner can raise questions about a particular content validation he can make an appropriate check upon the formal research involved.

Predictive validity uses an assumed state of affairs to judge current information. This form of validity is not concerned with why an event occurs; it does not attempt to relate content to reality. Predictive validity states that when one of two events occurs the other will also occur. If the number of babies increases when storks roost in chimneys, one event has predictive validity of the other and the lack of logical relationship between the two events is inconsequential. This form of validity is tenuous and only lasts as long as the events (observations of reality) continue in a set sequence.

Construct validity is perhaps the most comprehensive check of reality, and consequently the most controversial among researchers. Construct validity attempts to determine whether certain measures actually represent a particular conceptual idea. Are certain indicators which are stated to represent "aggression" in a particular piece of research valid? This is judged by the researcher using some other conceptual measure to test the predicted relationship of "aggression" and the concrete indicators. In other words, the researcher judges if the overt measures that mark one concept relate with some other concept that logically would seem to be in the same area. If "aggression" and "decision authority" have some logical similarities then the specific indicators used for both ideas have some overlap. Certain statistical techniques are available to measure the amount of overlap between specific indicators of concepts.

These are five of the most basic concepts necessary to understand the language of formal research. Others will be discussed in the following chapters about the specific operations of the formal research project.

Questions

1. What are the differences between independent and dependent variables?
2. What does multivariate analysis mean?
3. How do inferential and descriptive statistics differ?
4. How do parametric and non-parametric statistics differ?
5. What is a sample?
6. What is statistical significance?
7. What is variance? How does systematic variance differ from error variance?
8. What is reliability?
9. What are content, predictive, and construct validity?

7

Constructing a
Research Problem

When the practicing educator analyzes a piece of formal research, he must not overlook the vital importance of the construction phase. Construction of a research problem is perhaps the most difficult and important part of the whole process (1).

Based on the need identified in the search process which preceeds the formal research process, the problem is constructed through four major steps. They are shown in figure 14.

Figure 14   **The Construction Phase**

THEORY ⟶ DEFINED ⟶ OPERATIONAL ⟶ NULL
         PROBLEM   HYPOTHESIS   HYPOTHESIS

The construction phase is based on the concept of *deduction* (2). The thinker begins with a general awareness of his environment that is achieved by an inductive process and he carries out his search for some meaningful problem by this method. However, once the problem is identified the thought process is translated to one of deduction. Induction does not enter the formal process of research until the interpretation phase (3).

The deductive researcher works from a general explanation through logical links to a specific factual problem (4). He asks a series of "if . . . then" questions. "*If* this general statement is true, *then* this specific statement must follow from it." The key to deductive reasoning is the logical consistency of filling in the links between levels of abstraction. Deduction is the reasoning used in problem construction and the focus of problem construction is the hypothesis (5). Formal research predicts relationships between variables at all steps in construction of the problem.

The steps of construction

Constructing a problem in research is a hypothetic-deductive process that takes a general idea and brings it into the world of concrete fact. There are a series of steps, held together by logic and prediction, which form a "downward" ladder.

Three basic steps build most problems in educational research. These are the theoretical, conceptual, and operational translations. Often formal research contains a fourth step, the statistical prediction. Figure 15 illustrates these steps.

Figure 15   **Steps in Construction Phase**

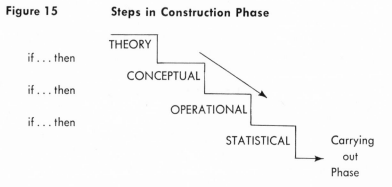

Theory

Theory is the most abstract level of the educational research problem. Theory is an explanation and prediction of relations that are believed to occur in the factual world (6). Theory is based on considerable information.

It is an abstract explanation which can be traced to actual facts by the two-way ladder of deductive and inductive logic. Some theories presume to explain a wider range of relationships than others; for example, a theory which accounts for people resolving role conflict is more general than a theory of how principals react to demands of teachers and the central office.

A theory also makes predictions. The presentation of the idea is designed so that implicit *cause and effect* relations are set up. The theoretical description which specifies relationships between variables is a most important point in problem construction. As the theory is transformed through the various steps into an operational hypothesis it is the *relationships* which are tested, not the variables (7). For example, predictive theory does not analyze "grouping procedures," "method of teaching," "age," or "years of experience." These variables mean nothing in theory unless predictive relations are specified between them. If the researcher presents the theoretical explanation, "aggression occurs when a person is frustrated in getting to his goals," it is the *action* relationship between goal and person which determines the ability to make research predictions (8).

Definition of the problem

The second step in construction is the problem statement or conceptual hypothesis. The initial form of the second step may be a question which arises directly from the theoretical explanation and which can provide us with a clue as to the logic of the researcher. The question should "flow" logically from the major variables and relationships of the theory step.

This second step in problem construction should also provide a conceptual prediction of the question. For example, if a researcher began with a theory about "aggression" and "a person," the second or conceptual step may refine these ideas in the educational context; aggression may become "hostile remarks to the principal" and a person may become the plural "teachers." The conceptual level is still too general for the researcher to test the prediction by concrete operations, but it does identify the specific variables and relationships which are to be made operational.

Most educational research actually begins at this conceptual level. The world of fact is changing so quickly that many explanations and predictions must be fairly specific; certainly in education we have nothing approaching the laws of physical science. Although the practitioner finds many principles in education, these are often value judgments rather than logically consistent derivatives of present-day facts. Formal research which begins with an educational question rather than a general theory is acceptable when the conceptual prediction about the problem is also given. Jumping from a conceptual question to a third-step operational prediction, however, would violate explanation or theory building, which is the ultimate goal of science (9). In other words, no matter at which level formal research is carried out it should begin with a comprehensive explanation of the problem.

The operational hypothesis

The operational step is the third level of construction. This step restates the conceptual prediction in terms of *specific* observations, measures, conditions, and operations necessary to carry out the research. The operational step outlines the research design (see chapter 8) and specifies concrete methods to test the problem. It restates the hypothesis in the specific relations between variables which are to be tested.

The null hypothesis

The fourth step of problem construction may or may not occur in formal research. This is the statistical prediction or *null hypothesis* (written H_0 in statistical formulas). The statistical hypothesis reverses the operational prediction and tests for *no difference*. Notice that the null hypothesis does not add to or detract from the operational description of the variables or relationships under study. In effect, it is a test of whether the differences in a study are real or just the result of chance (10). To accomplish this test the null hypothesis predicts that there is no difference.

The educator may ask why it is necessary to put the operational prediction in this form. For the moment, think of the statistical prediction of no difference as providing a mathematical standard by which to judge quantifiable information. The null hypothesis is a statement of equality, chosen independently, that sets the amount of difference which is considered statistically acceptable and the amount which must be rejected. If the test of *no* difference is *accepted*, the researcher knows his data *falls below* the statistical standard set to represent actual difference. If the null hypothesis is *rejected,* the researcher knows he *has* actual statistical difference.

Consistency of the construction steps

A concrete example of the steps involved in taking a research problem from theory to null hypothesis may help us see the logical consistency of the deductive process in transformation (11). Here the topic of "aggression" is translated by formal research construction.

1. Theory Step:
   Aggression occurs when a person is frustrated in getting to his goals. Whenever a person is prevented from getting what he wants, an urge induces him to behave aggressively toward the party responsible for his frustration.
2. Conceptual Step: (Question form optional)
   Teachers prevented from participating in committee decision-making with the principal will express greater hostility in their remarks to the principal during the school day than teachers not prevented from participating in committee decision-making with the principal.
3. Operational Step:
   The ratio of "hostile" to "non-hostile" remarks that are classified as "directed toward principal," based on observation of verbal interaction by four trained observers during 8:00 A.M. to 3:30 P.M. of two school days, will be significantly lower under condition A (randomly chosen teachers of Smith High School allowed to vote in committee decision-making) than under condition B (randomly chosen teachers of Smith High School not allowed to vote in committee decision-making).

Notice the word "significantly" in the operational step. This tells the reader that a fourth step of construction has been added, the statistical prediction. An example of the same aggression problem at the fourth step of statistical prediction shows how that step is handled.

4a. Statistical Step:
   The proportion of hostile remarks among teachers under conditions A will be equal to that in condition B.

The educator may see the above statistical prediction of no difference written in the following manner:

b. 1. $H_0 = \text{Teachers}_A = \text{Teachers}_B$ or $T_A - T_B = 0$
   2. $\alpha = 0.05$
   3. Reject H_0 if $\chi^2 > 0.05 = $ statistically significant value

These symbols provide a shorthand way to tell the researcher the null hypothesis that is to be examined *and* the means by which to do the testing. In this statement $\propto$ means the level of significance, $>$ means "greater than" (the symbol $<$ means "less than"), 0.05 means that rejection of the null hypothesis occurs when the results could not have occurred by chance more than 5 in 100 times. The "statistically significant value" is determined from a mathematical table for the specified level of significance when the researcher uses a certain statistic with a particular problem. χ^2 is the symbol for the chi square statistic; chi square is used to compare proportions of frequency scores against chance.

The above two forms of the null hypothesis tell the same message. There are statistically set limits which determine if there is actual difference in teachers found in conditions A and B (12). If teachers responded so differently that they could be considered a group separate from the general population, the null hypothesis would be rejected. Interpretation will be further discussed in chapter 11.

Analysis of construction

The practitioner can ask crucial questions about problem construction without becoming involved with the minute details of formal research.

A most critical question concerns what was left out or added at each step or restatement of the problem. How well the researcher "moved down" the ladder depends on the "tightness" of his logic. The logical connection of the various steps is all-important. Remember that the theory or conceptual steps are not actually tested in a constructed problem; it is the operational level that is tested directly. If statistics are used, the null hypothesis is the only step of the ladder actually tested. The potential danger of misinterpretation when problem construction rests on the statistical prediction alone is obvious.

For example, suppose that in a given problem the null hypothesis is rejected, and a researcher finds a statistically significant difference. First, he must infer if the found difference was caused by the conditions he was studying. Perhaps the difference occurred because of variables outside the problem as it was constructed. The statistical step represents the theoretical problem only if the variables and tested relationships are represented accurately. It is this representation that must be closely scrutinized, *not* just the statistical "proofs."

A closer look at the example about aggression demonstrates specific questions that the practitioner may ask to determine good problem construction in formal research.

Translation and terminology

Major questions at the abstract levels revolve around translation and terminology. The practitioner may ask two questions:
1. Does the translation of terms progress logically from theory, to concept, to operational prediction?
2. Are the conceptual terms specific enough?

The problem was defined in this way at the most abstract level: Aggression occurs when a person is frustrated in getting to his goals. Whenever a person is prevented from getting what he wants, an urge induces him to behave aggressively toward the party responsible for his frustration.

In the example, "aggression" was defined as a behavioral act resulting from an "urge" caused by frustration. A practical question here is whether aggression is only caused by a generalized "urge" of frustration. Adler, the famous psychologist, talks of aggression as *any* manifestation toward a "will-to-power." Was Hitler's attack on Poland solely a result of "power" frustration? Sigmund Freud states aggression results from a personal "death instinct." If these are viable alternative explanations of aggression, then consideration of the problem in theory may not be complete.

A second basic question of terminology concerns the meaning of "behaving aggressively toward" the party responsible for the frustration. Behavior can be direct or indirect. Direct action may take many forms, from emotional outbursts to physical abuse; indirect behavior can be displaced toward people or objects that are not the original source of frustration. Does the theory explain and predict types of aggressive action toward others?

Finally, does the explanation specify "the party responsible"? Aggression can be turned inward; the extreme form of internal agression is suicide. Does the theory cover this meaning?

Obviously, we can think of many other questions about terminology in the aggression example. The point is, formal research theory may offer an explanation which is not a well-thought-out generalization, and probing questions can disclose any weaknesses in the explanation.

The second "step" was conceptual:

Teachers prevented from participation in committee decision-making with the principal will express greater hostility in their remarks to the principal during the school day than teachers not prevented from participating in committee decision-making with the principal.

If the conceptual step is appropriate, the research problem should specify and answer many questions about how terminology of the theoretical explanation is interpreted in an educational context. In this example, frustration is said to be caused by prevention of the teachers from participating with the principal in committee decision-making. Aggression, resulting from teacher frustration, is characterized by hostile remarks made during the school day.

The "person frustrated" in the explanation level is transformed into the "teachers" at the conceptual step and the "party responsible" is interpreted as "the principal". The "prevented" goal becomes "participation in committee decision-making" and "aggressive behavior" is now interpreted as hostile remarks.

In this example the translation of many terms from theory to concept seems logical enough. However, there are words which still are vague or unexplained.

Can all "teachers" be considered similar? Do teachers differ whether they teach elementary or secondary school, whether they are older than 35 or not, and whether they have academic or vocational interests? If any of these characteristics differentiate people in regard to their participation, then the term "teacher" is too vague.

Does the research problem tell what "participating in committee decision-making" means? Participation may range from giving advice to making final decisions. A committee may contain the principal and one teacher, a number of teachers only, or many other combinations. Decisions may cover matters that range from throwing trash on school grounds to teacher censorship. These factors may all affect meaning.

In this way the practitioner can apply the logical questioning of terms and their translation to any specific operations. He can judge the soundness of logic, hypothesis construction, and definition of the more general steps.

The operational step should predict an outcome in specific, testable, form. Translation from the conceptual level should be logically consistent, should spell out relationships to be tested, and should specify terms. The operational hypothesis should be capable of direct measurement.

Our example gave the following operational hypothesis:

The ratio of "hostile" to "non-hostile" remarks that are classified as "directed toward principal," based on observation of verbal interaction by four trained observers during 8:00 A.M. to 3:30 P.M. of two school days, will be significantly lower under condition A (randomly chosen teachers of Smith High School allowed to vote in committee decision-making) than under condition B (randomly chosen teachers of Smith High School not allowed to vote in committee decision-making).

The relationship to be tested was the observed ratio of certain remarks in condition A to those in condition B during a specified period of time. Remarks were verbal, either "hostile" or "non-hostile," and directed toward the principal. They were identified by four trained observers. The "school day" was a time period from 8:00 A.M. to 3:30 P.M. Teachers and principals belonged to Smith High School. "Participation" in decision-making was specified to mean voting. A possible deficiency of the operational terminology was the failure to identify "committee."

The operational step in constructing a research problem specifies procedures to carry out formal research. Practical methods for assessing the data-gathering and analytical procedures and the terms within an overall research design will be covered in the following three chapters.

The final step in the ladder of constructing the "aggression" example was the statistical hypothesis.

The example gave the following statistical prediction of no difference:

The proportion of hostile remarks among teachers under conditions A will be equal to that in condition B.

Some questionable areas for translation at this level are the use of the chi square statistic, the sample size, and whether .05 level of significance is appropriate. These questions will be discussed in the chapters on analysis and interpretation.

The prediction

The steps of problem construction also give the practitioner an opportunity to analyze the essential ingredients of the prediction. All hypotheses must follow certain "rules" in formal research. The various predictions must have:

1. two or more variables; usually an independent (indicated X) and dependent (indicated Y) type.
2. the predicted relations between variables specified.

The two or more variables in a hypothesis must share the same general subject. If a particular researcher is predicting whether "democratic" behavior of teachers makes students more "democratic," there may be confusion about the general subject; does the researcher measure the teachers' actions and the students' reactions by the same criteria? Democratic behavior may acquire two different meanings in the carrying-out phase of research, and thus the variables may not in fact share a common subject.

The difference between dependent and independent variables must be specified. Remember that the dependent variable *depends* on changes or variations in the independent variable.

The final check of variables in a prediction consists of analyzing the type of differences which can be expected. A variable can vary in *kind* or in *degree*. When a variable can be divided into categories it differs in kind. Autocratic or democratic is an example of difference in kind. The same is true with male or female, and with blue, brown, or black eyes. The other type of variable difference is by degree. Anything that can be counted within a single category differs by degree; for example, a person's age or the number of hostile remarks are variables which differ by degree. The caution point for practicing educators is to check the variables which differ in *kind*. In our example of "aggression," the committee participation is such a variable that is highly suspect.

The second area where the practicing educator should check the prediction or hypothesis is the relationship between variables.

The hypothesis should state precisely how variation of the independent variables is supposed to affect the dependent variable. Variables can vary in either a *direct* or *inverse* relationship. For example, achievement and IQ scores are variables which can form several different relationships. The researcher can set the prediction to state that as one goes up the other goes up or that as one goes down the other follows suit. This is a direct relationship between variables; an inverse relationship would predict that when achievement goes up IQ goes down, or visa versa.

Once variables and relationships are identified, the practitioner should check the hypotheses of problem construction to insure that the following specific mistakes have *not* been made:

1. *Stating only one variable.* The statement "school board members are mainly business men" contains only one variable.
2. *Not stating how variation is expected to occur.* "A teacher's personality is a function of student discipline problems" does not specify the occurrence of variation.

3. *Stating a relationship between variables as a question rather than a prediction.* The conceptual step must go beyond such a question as "will teachers be more likely to express hostile attitudes?"

4. *Stating only the existence of a relationship between variables.* The hypothesis must describe a directed or expected relationship between variables. The prediction, "pupil-teacher ratio influences the teacher job satisfaction" is not a valid hypothesis because it does not contain such a description.

Any of these mistakes in problem construction can ruin a piece of formal research. The practitioner can be a highly discriminating judge of the adequacy of research if he focusses upon translation, terms, and prediction.

The intuitive analysis

No doubt the practicing educator can also see the possibility of judging formal research in an intuition-oriented manner. Intuitive thinking means directing personal experiences or feelings of what is right to the specific aspects of formal research. The practitioner's goal is either to recognize good research or to ask intelligent questions. The intuitive approach may be directed to all phases of the formal research process.

A person's experience and ability to think logically can often counteract a lack of expertise. Analysis of formal research can be accomplished without extensive background or training. Although the practitioner is not expected to master the intricacies of research he can identify checkpoints to distinguish acceptable research and can gain a healthy skepticism of questionable areas.

As we have seen in this chapter the practitioner is generally on equal footing with the researcher in the construction of a problem. Educational research does not control the market on logical consistency. The practicing educator's judgment on how well the word aggression is represented by the terms "hostility" or "overt hostile remarks" is just as valid as that of the researcher who constructed the relationship between words. If the researcher cannot demonstrate that he proceeded consistently from general theory to a null hypothesis, the practitioner is under no obligation to accept the rationale of his formal research. The deductive links between steps must make sense, the specific terms tested at the operational level must flow from the abstract concepts and terminology, the relationships between variables must translate smoothly from the general to the specific steps, and the predictions must meet the criteria of "good" hypotheses. The construction phase of formal research is especially oriented to the practitioner's judgment, for there are few rules of analysis beyond personal intuition about what is logical in the areas of terminology, translation, and prediction.

Questions

1. What are the steps in the construction phase of formal research?
2. How does the process of deduction affect theory building?
3. How is the hypothesis used in the operational step?
4. What is the null hypothesis?
5. What is statistical significance and how does it relate to problem construction?
6. What are some major questions in the construction of
     a) theory building?
     b) hypothesis setting?
7. What is the intuitive approach to analyzing formal research?

8

The Research Design

The intuitive approach to analyzing formal research is also feasible in the "carrying-out" phase, the overall plan for which is called the research design. This design lays out the way that formal research is to be carried out and outlines detailed descriptions of the research variables and procedures. The research design flows from the operational hypothesis, which was defined in the construction phase; if a research problem is properly constructed the hypothesis predetermines the design framework. A research design accounts for 1) what is studied, 2) the subjects involved, 3) methods of collecting data, 4) methods of analyzing data, and 5) the method of drawing conclusions (1).

There are many kinds of research designs and consequently a confusing number of different types of formal research. However, designs can be classified by certain common threads which the practitioner can easily recognize.

All designs can be categorized initially as either looking-back or right-now types. The reason for the non-scientific titles used is to emphasize one of the greatest distinctions in research designs — the time perspective. Looking-back designs study educational problems through a historical perspective of variables and their relationships; the events considered have already occurred. Right-now designs deal with present, on-going, or future educational situations.

A second distinguishing quality of research designs is *control*. What is controlled and how it is, identifies various types of design.

The question of control may be confusing. Research at the turn of this century was often little more than one person's interpretation and description of a general situation; such efforts were called naturalistic studies (2). If this type of study is considered formal research then designs are possible without specific controls, for the design becomes each person's individual view of the world. But most current educational research demands the use of controls when we study an area of interest. Assuming that control is necessary, research designs differ in *what* control is achieved, and it is therefore possible to subdivide both the designs for study of the past and those of the present according to the controls needed.

Practically all designs in formal research attempt some form of *focus controls,* and consequently focus controls cannot be used to distinguish types of design. These controls are intended to keep the specific research design focused upon the specific event that is being studied. But on the other hand, the types of *environmental controls* used, or their lack of use, can be used to classify both looking-back and right-now designs. (Environmental control, which is concerned with unwanted variables, may or may not be used.) The schematic illustration in figure 16, which shows how designs differ, may clarify the distinctions.

Figure 16

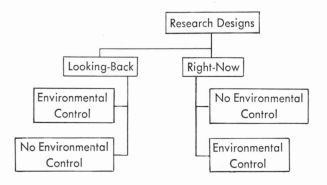

After the focus of control is determined the practitioner should assess *how* control is to be achieved.

Right-now designs use *physical* controls of variables; the researcher actually manipulates the conditions under study before or during the conduct of research. Physical controls are often applied to environmental variables which may impinge on a particular study. For example, a researcher may study only males to "control" for the intervening influences of sex. Physical manipulation of the environment in a study using a right-now design usually demands the use of control groups and statistics. The practitioner must be especially careful in assessing the use of statistics in a research design. Some right-now designs use *statistics to support physical manipulation* of variables, but looking-back designs may use *statistics to approximate facts* or events which have already occurred.

Physical manipulation may also occur in the focus of a right-now design. This is called *the treatment* of the problem and it usually contains some researcher-imposed change of the independent variable. For example, to study a new teaching method the researcher could set up a teaching situation, impose the new method (treatment), and then assess change in the situation.

Because looking-back designs deal with events which have passed, it is not possible to control physically the variables involved. This is a crucial distinction in *how* looking-back designs differ from present-situation designs. The looking-back design relies on *logical* or *statistical* control of the variables and relationships under study.

The statistical researcher uses mathematical techniques to remove unwanted effects and to approximate the conditions of an ongoing research environment. The logical researcher attempts to control unwanted factors in a backward-looking situation by constructing a valid picture of past reality from a present-day starting point; this process is controlled by the two-way process of deduction and induction.

In summary, the practicing educator has an initial way to judge the carrying-out phase of formal research. The research design can be classified according to several criteria:

1. The time perspective of the study.
2. Whether environmental or unwanted variables are controlled.
3. Whether control of variables is by physical, logical or statistical methods.

Common right-now designs

Right-now designs which include environmental control are called experimental designs. An experimental design has 1) physical control of the research environment, 2) a "treatment" phase, and 3) subsequent observation of the treatment effect. Some researchers would add randomization of the groups being studied as critical for a true experimental design (3).

The educator can look for the following characteristics in a good experimental design:

1. At least two sample groups of people being studied. One group will receive the "treatment" and is normally called the *experimental* group. The other sample will receive no treatment and will be referred to as the *control* group. There may be more than one experimental and control group, depending on how elaborate the specific experimental design is.
2. The people in the various samples may be assigned by a randomization procedure. If the people are not assigned randomly the design may be referred to as *pre-experimental or quasi-experimental* (4).
3. Some form of "treatment" will be given. The group or groups designated as experimental will be manipulated in some manner.
4. There will be an observation after the treatment. The control and experimental groups will be compared for logical relationships in terms of the hypothesis.

Notice that the effect of the treatment phase is the central focus of this type of right-now design. Without the physically imposed treatment the experiment could not take place. An illustration of a true experimental design is given in figure 17.

Figure 17

Groups	Research Observation	Treatment Phase	Research Observation
Randomly assigned experimental group	Pre-treatment observation	Treatment performed	Post-treatment observation
Randomly assigned control group	Pre-treatment observation	No treatment	Post-treatment observation

The basic question to be answered in the experimental situation is whether the treatment phase made a difference between the experimental and control groups.

Modifications of the right-now design may add more experimental and control groups or may eliminate the pre-treatment observations; treatment may also be simulated rather than actually given to some control groups. The educator who is interested in the type of true experimental designs available to the researcher should refer to David C. Campbell and Julian C. Stanley's *Experimental and Quasi-Experimental Designs for Research.*

There are many other examples of right-now designs in educational research (5). Normally these are not true experimental designs because they lack certain controls.

The Laboratory Experiment

An educational study which can be carried out in a laboratory is a form of research where variables are tightly controlled and an artificial situation is created. The attempt is made to isolate the problem from unintended influences, a difficult thing to do when research concerns people. The laboratory is used to obtain the highest degree of control possible. Laboratory experiments can be easily identified in the research literature; the demand for control of the situation forces this type of study to 1) create the variables to be tested for effect and 2) build an artificial situation to control variables which are not the concern of the researcher.

As an example of a laboratory experiment we could bring two groups of high school administrators to a university to participate in a research study, having selected both groups randomly so that we can assume they are similar. On arrival, members of the groups are tested for desire to be a metropolitan superintendent. The groups then are put in a three day workshop on the superintendency, using the same instructors and material. In addition, one group is subjected to a "treatment": reading a carefully constructed newspaper filled with negative stories about big-city living and urban educational problems which present a hopeless future for metropolitan superintendents. At the end of the workshop, we again test members of the two groups on their desire for superintendency.

Beyond the admitted limitations of this hypothetical study, we see the rationale of laboratory experiments in education. The subjects are removed from their natural educational setting, they are manipulated by the researchers during the study, and the results are drawn from an analysis of change within a carefully controlled framework.

The Field Experiment

The field experiment is a modification of the laboratory experimental study. A major difference in the field experiment is that it is carried out in the natural setting. The researcher manipulates the variables he is studying but does not try to control all unintended influences in the environment. The same example of principals being tested on their desire for superintendency could be adapted to a field experiment. In this case two groups of practicing local school administrators would be identified and tested for desire while on the job, one group would then be given the newspapers, and both would subsequently be tested.

The field experiment has advantages and disadvantages when compared to the laboratory experiment. Although there is a loss of control for outside influences which adds difficulty in replication of the study, the field is more realistic and lifelike. Principals brought to a laboratory setting may be more likely to plan games to fool the researcher. Secondly, the interacting influences, processes, and changes surrounding the urban principalship or superintendency are too complex to be approximated in a laboratory workshop.

External and Internal Validity

The right-now type of research design must face certain questions of external and internal validity (6). These allow the practicing educator further opportunity to make an intuitive assessment of the research design.

The ongoing study or design itself must be analyzed for consistency with its stated purposes. If the research problem dictates that the design has randomized assignment of participants then randomization becomes an internal-validity problem. Another internal-validity question might be whether the instrument used to gather information is administered correctly. If an instrument is not filled out (questionnaires particularly have a peculiar habit of disappearing into educators' waste baskets) or filled out incorrectly the study and research design have low internal validity.

If the researcher wants to do more than merely describe the results of what was observed he must be concerned with external validity. The external validity tests involve the relationship of the designed study to outside reality. External validity centers on the question of generalization; randomization of study participants is crucial for external validity because it is the key to generalization. The researcher who does not build the randomization technique into his research design can not infer his found results based on the study.

In effect, external validity is determined by the relationship of the design to the researcher's purpose. Most violations of external validity occur in the creation of the research design; once it is created, most violations of internal validity occur in its improper implementation.

All research designs must demonstrate internal validity. In the experimental design, internal validity hinges on whether the treatment made an actual difference. Possible areas where flaws in the internal validity might occur are 1) the selection of groups being studied (the control group and the experiment group), 2) changes during the time of the experiment, and 3) instruments used to measure difference.

Suppose a researcher created a design to study the effect of a new teaching device upon the learning of children. The first problem of internal validity would be choosing the people to be studied; who would make up the comparison groups? If the children were different to begin with, any difference caused by the treatment (teaching device) might be biased.

A second problem is the possibility of changes in the selected children during the experiment (e.g., did the children grow mentally?). Sixth graders, for example, are different at the beginning and end of the school year.

A final problem in internal validity of right-now designs is the method of observing and measuring effect. Did the treatment change children in the experimental group in other ways than what was measured? Did the children know, and act as though, they were in a special situation?

Certain right-now designs, those which attempt to generalize results, also face problems of external validity. In the example, once the results were obtained how much can they be generalized to fit all children? Factors affecting the external validity of experimental designs are 1) the specific relationship of the people in the experiment to the variables being studied, 2) the particular setting of the experiment, and 3) the possible effects of testing.

An extreme illustration of a problem between people and the variables under study would be analyzing the use of computer-assisted instruction to teach pre-kindergarten students spelling. Obviously, if the children had not learned the alphabet the computer would have limited validity as a teaching device.

The particular setting of a study may affect the external validity of an experiment. A conscious effort to analyze the extent of the setting was made in the famous Western Electric Studies (7). In this effort certain physical variables in the organizational environment, particularly the lighting, were manipulated to analyze the effect upon the output of telephone workers. Researchers may inadvertently create a special setting and then attempt to generalize from it to the normal state of affairs; children's learning in a laboratory, for example, may have poor external validity when generalized to the school classroom.

Testing may bias the external validity. If testing procedures involve a unique situation which can not be replicated, the lack of reliability hampers claims of external validity. Educators know intuitively that children in Toronto, Ontario, will differ somewhat from children in Harlem, New York, in Greenwood, Mississippi, or in Palo Alto, California. Testing procedures which can not be replicated in each of these locations to determine the extent of difference negate the application of research results from a particular study.

This is only an example of the many questions surrounding the internal and external validity of right-now research designs. An educator dealing with normal research needs to understand some of the possible pitfalls in this type of design.

Common looking-back designs

The looking-back research design deals with facts after they have occurred. The research does not create an effect through a treatment phase. Looking-back designs will normally consist of two stages: 1) observation or gathering of facts and 2) logical or statistical interpretation of relationships. An example of looking-back research is given in figure 18.

Figure 18

Obtaining information   Statistical interpretation
on existing variables ⟶ of relationships

The major question mark in this type of design is how facts are obtained. Statistical techniques help justify the internal validity of research results once facts have been gathered, but the basic question of what constitutes a fact remains. The looking-back design assumes data to be quantifiable facts, depending on previously established information to handle the initial questions of internal validity, but the design may not in actuality have control over the creation or quantification of facts. The instruments used to gather data and the judgments on numerical scoring may be accepted as given. If a looking-back researcher is given scores for IQ, teacher attitudes, age, philosophical orientation, and political affiliation, he may interpret the internal validity of difference or relationships through statistics or logic, but the fundamental question about the facts themselves remains.

The external validity of looking-back designs rests with the ability of the researcher to generalize findings. Generalization rests on 1) the validity of factual data analyzed and 2) the ability to apply the specific relationships found to other situations that have the same variables.

One common looking-back design is the field study, a historical look at relationships of the past which can tell something about the present social world. The variables studied are taken from real life situations, not ones constructed by the researcher. A field study accounts for the relationships, behaviors, attitudes, perceptions, or values in a social system.

The hypothesis-testing field study is adaptable to the formal looking-back research design. This type of field study gathers information about a situation and assesses whether a prediction is supported by the facts. There is rapidly growing use of this type of field study in educational research as the result of increased sophistication in statistics and other substitutes for physical controls.

For an example, consider a hypothesis-testing field study of the desires of principals to become superintendents. The information that is gathered on a random sample of local school administrators would include analysis of each person's desire for the superintendency, plus other physical, organizational, and attitudinal variables. The researcher would then set "desire" as the dependent variable and statistically analyze the effect of such things as age, years of experience, present size of local school, location, and feelings about education. In effect, the hypothesis-testing field study predicts the amount of difference that each social variable might cause on the desire variable.

In addition to questions of validity in both right-now and looking-back designs, the practitioner should check two final aspects. The different forms of research designs carry social and methodological implications which affect the cause-effect relations and the research process.

Social implications

The right-now designs must consider social consequences in the use of physical controls. Using the design in social research does not give the freedom of manipulating conditions that is usually enjoyed by the physical scientist. The educational researcher makes a critical value judgment when he controls conditions prior to or during an experiment; some degree of social artificiality is entered. The researchers must ask what stipulations are necessary for the real world if people are controlled. The physical control of temperature or light in a laboratory is a simple research problem, but the manipulation of humans involves an additional moral judgment.

On the other hand, the looking-back design is subject to the researcher's bias or preference. By selection of the variables that are to be considered and the relationships that are under study, a slanted picture of the social world may be created. In effect, the researcher's choice of what makes up the design re-creates his interpretation of the past.

Methodological implications

The type of research design chosen plays a large part in determining the specific way information is analyzed. The use of statistical techniques is an example. Certain research designs require assumptions about the dependent variable that determine some of the statistical assumptions and methods used to control unwanted variables. A few examples are in order to show how a specific type of statistic is often tied to a particular research design (8).

Correlation and regression are two statistical techniques which aid the researcher in analyzing the relationships between facts or variables. These techniques are often used in looking-back designs because they are concerned with events that have occurred. Correlation deals with the question, once X and Y have occurred, as to what is the relationship between them. Another way of stating the purpose of correlation is to analyze the *strength* represented by the linear relationship between a pair of variables. Regression questions ask how much variance in the dependent variable can be accounted for by the varying of the independent variable.

Correlation and regression techniques also have modifications which statistically control unwanted facts after they have taken place. This means physical control of variables may be avoided. Although correlation and regression can be used in all designs they are highly adaptable to a historical context.

The right-now design is more oriented to statistical methods such as the analysis of variance. Analysis of variance demands an isolation of the variables to be studied. The conditions have to be controlled because analysis of variance is concerned with change *within* both X and Y as well as between them. The educator can see that the use of this statistical technique depends on design control of both the situation and unwanted effects over a period of time. Although applicable to looking-back studies, analysis of variance is so effective in analyzing a research situation over a given time that it often is used with right-now designs.

Which design is superior?

Research in education is directly affected by people and social organizations. This raises the fundamental question of which design in best for the purpose of approaching reality in a social situation.

Right-now designs grew from the researchers' desire for assurance of concrete reality. The classical scientific method used in the physical sciences seemed to present a convincing argument; if research could physically keep unwanted elements from bothering the situation that was under study there could be a more positive analysis of gathered information. Physical-science research fostered the desire of social researchers to become "respectable." The social sciences were considered messy compared to the physical sciences, and some members of the intellectual community seemed to have a condescending attitude toward the subjective nature of social research.

Historically, right-now preceeded looking-back designs in social research. The impact of the physical sciences, the relative lack of statistical sophistication, and the inability to handle large amounts of information before the computer all contributed to this fact. In the early days of social research the alternatives to right-now design with strict physical control were historical studies with no control or, at most, logical control. Consequently, research dealing after the fact (called ex-post-facto) was not generally accepted, and often, ex-post-facto research is still equated with early social surveys and descriptive studies which characteristically contained high degrees of bias, unsophisticated data collection, weak analysis, and dubious results.

It is not surprising that many social researchers still attach the stigma of ex-post-facto research to present day looking-back designs. A reputation is hard to outlive.

However, current looking-back designs have drastically increased in degree of research sophistication. The reasons are the use of statistical controls and the ability of the computer to simultaneously handle massive amounts of information about past events.

Statistical looking-back designs are based on the premise that all social research approximates the real world, which consists of existing factual information. A design should attempt to approximate reality by statistically controlling facts rather than physically entering social situations. In effect, these looking-back designs statistically remove the social facts to be studied from the rest of the past real-life environment.

The question of which type of design is "best" remains unanswered. Certainly we can judge the relative sophistication of the control mechanisms, but perhaps the best answer is that the specific educational situation or problem to be studied determines which design is superior. The laboratory experiment is the research ideal but it is not always feasible.

The question of cause and effect

A final point distinguishes the right-now from the looking-back research design. This is the question of inferring cause and effect relationships among the variables under study. Researchers using either type of design will never talk in an absolute or deterministic manner about something causing a reaction or a variable that is effected by another. Research results are always tentative and subject to error. The research design is created to add confidence in the handling of information and thus in the results. However, the looking-back design differs from the right-now design in the manner that the confidence is created and inferred. Certainty in results with right-now research designs is approached by the process of elimination. The situation under study is controlled and analyzed within a particular design framework. The found results are then re-tested with the same type of controls to see if the subsequent results are similar. A modification of right-now design retesting is a changing of physical controls to analyze the difference from initial results caused by the alteration. In both cases, right-now designs are used for elimination of alternate explanations to the initial results. The active process of retesting and manipulation is the primary device for inferring cause and effect.

The looking-back design does not have the manipulation alteration and re-test abilities enjoyed by the right-now research situation.

Cause and effect relationships are inferred from the found results of given facts. The inability to recheck alternate explanations drawn from modified conditions is a serious weakness in looking-back designs.

In effect, the two designs differ in the type of reanalysis that is possible to gather confidence about cause and effect results. A further discussion of cause and effect relationships is found in Chapter 11 on interpretation and conclusions.

Questions

1. What is the purpose of a research design?
2. What are the major distinctions between a right-now and looking-back design?
3. How does a design differentiate the statistic used?
4. What is the treatment?
5. What are the differences between experimental and quasi-experimental designs?
6. What is a field experiment and how does it differ from a field study?
7. How are right-now designs affected by internal and external validity?
8. What are the social and methodological implications associated with use of different types of designs?
9. What is "cause and effect"?

9

Collecting Information

Data collection is occasionally described as the "lost" portion of formal research. Educational researchers sometimes seem to be divided into two literary camps, the theory writers and the "hard-data" men. Theory writers spend most of their effort constructing logical and comprehensive explanations of educational problems; specific factual information seems included as a supporting aside.

"Hard data" writers concentrate on the analysis of information. They seem not as concerned with the general context of information as with the manipulative and analytical hoops that data can be made to jump through. This brand of research writing bursts at the seams with sophisticated analytical techniques and esoteric numerical results.

Somewhere between the concepts of theory and the analysis of facts lies the question of what constitutes "information" or "facts" in the first place. Three critical questions continually nag proponents of either extreme position: 1) what is factual information, 2) how is the information gathered, and 3) who provides the information (1)?

The "who, what, and how" questions define the information studied.

The practicing educator should consider how a piece of research answers these questions to analyze the real merit of any writing. If questions are not answered satisfactorily, no theoretical construct or amount of statistical reordering will save a study.

What is collected?

What are used as data for a particular study depends on certain basic "rules." When certain factual information is gathered for any study it is an *indicator,* not an actual representation of the idea (2). Many ideas that educators are concerned with, such as child hostility, staff morale, or administrative leadership cannot be observed as "hard fact"; researchers must infer these ideas by identifying characteristics of presumed indicators. For example, one child hitting another may point to "hostility"; it is the researcher's indicator of the idea of hostility. Of course, some things are more obvious indicators of reality than others. For instance, sex or skin color — physical properties — are more easily identified than leadership — a psychological property.

In formal research the indicators of an idea must be observable to the researcher. This means that a researcher cannot determine "good morale" by looking for "happy" people, but one indicator of morale could be "smiling" because it is an observable indicator.

We may ask, "isn't there a lot of subjective choice about what indications represent an idea?" The answer of course is yes. The key to whether the choice is good or not depends on logic and how closely the indicator fits reality. For example, using "smile" as an indicator of positive morale raises the question of whether *all* smiles are similar. Do they always represent a positive response? A valid indicator of an idea must represent only one thing; smiling to be valid must always represent positive responses. This is not necessarily so, as a conversation indicated between two young boys who were describing their fifth-grade teacher:

"She smiles all the time."

"Yes, but so does a shark."

A second criterion for a good indicator is that another indicator of the opposite meaning must also be identifiable. If smiling indicates positive morale what is the opposite indicator which represents negative morale?

An indicator of any idea meets three criteria:

1. It is physically observable (smile).
2. It can only mean one thing (positive).
3. There is an identifiable opposite (negative gesture).

The researcher has *defined* and *classified* an idea (3). Both are critical in determining what information is to be collected in research. To actually analyze information collected in research, the educator must judge the information-gathering devices, a process that centers on the direct questioning of what tangible things represent an abstract idea and that must also consider item analysis and test construction (4).

How is information collected?

The second related question in collecting information is the method by which it is to be done. Once indicators are agreed upon, *how* are they collected? The two basic methods are by direct personal observation or through some written device; of course, the type of indicators that represent the idea determine what method is used to collect data. For example, "smiling" is best determined by direct observation while "handwriting skill" is best determined through written expression. Within both written and direct-observation methods there are many considerations which further determine how information is collected.

Formal research uses five common forms of information collection: interview, questionnaire, test, observation, and content analysis. With the exception of the questionnaire and written test, all forms use both a person and a written device to gather information and make judgments about indicators.

The *items* that are contained in written instruments must be analyzed to determine what indicators really are being collected. There are many pitfalls in making and using written indicators to collect information. The focus of an item, for example, is often not a correct representation of a particular indicator. If a child hitting someone is an indicator of "hostility" the item must be focused on the child; it may be "hostility" if viewed from the perspective of a child hitting an adult, but may also be "amusement" if judged by the response of the adult.

Other limits to written items often overlooked in research are "unknown," "unimportant," and "secret" information. Some items ask for information unknown to the respondent; if a questionnaire is given to 100 teachers and only 3 have information which lets them understand a particular item, the item is faulty. The guess responses of 97 teachers answering a question probably will cover up the three valid responses. Other misleading items pick up "unimportant information"; if a respondent is asked "what specific percentage of time is spent thinking about educational problems?" he may respond with a guess; few people can analyze themselves in specific percentages. An item which asks for "secret" information — material the respondent feels he should not divulge — may not receive honest answers; if the item is a threat the respondent may not answer at all.

Because questionnaires and written tests involve the perception of a respondent about an item, physical rather than psychological indicators should be used whenever possible. It is far easier for a respondent to give a written response about sex or eye color than "the number of authoritarian acts a principal makes."

Construction of written instruments has drawn the increasing attention of researchers. Construction is not easy, and developing a single item to collect information involves time and effort; a person constructing an item must consider motivation of the respondent, significance of the question, pertinence to the respondent's situation, simplicity of response, phrasing, and possible pre-coding (5). In addition, there are fundamental decisions to be made about "closed" versus "open-ended" items; closed items are easier to score but have to assume that all people are knowledgeable about the subject and no barriers exist in communication. A related item question involves the decision about "neutral" or "forced" choice; researchers are divided on the benefit of including "may or may not" and "cannot answer" categories in response choices. Neutral categories give a person who lacks information or who has no opinion a valid choice, but also provide a haven for those respondents who do not want to face the question.

These are some of the problems surrounding instrument construction (6). Gathering information by written instruments is risky. The educator trying to analyze the value of research that uses written instruments must put a question mark opposite collection unless there is a full description of the instrument.

Many written tests are well-known to practicing educators as means of collecting information. Some of them have been given to enough people to permit development of standardized item scores. A certain score may be designated the norm or average of a population and be expected to vary with the type of people tested. For example, a written test on spelling achievement may have a fifth-grade, seventh-grade, and ninth-grade norm for each item. There are standardized written tests on achievement, attitudes, behaviors, perceptions and so forth. Three questions must be applied to any written tests when they are used in formal research as methods of gathering information: 1) what, in specific indicators, is the instrument testing, 2) how was the instrument constructed, and 3) what is the possibility of bias entering the research because subject responses cannot be verified?

Because written instruments frequently have brought low returns and a high percentage of incorrectly filled-out items, much formal research uses a combination of person and written instrument to collect information. One of the best known combinations is the in-depth interview (7). A questionnaire form (called a schedule) is administered to a respondent by an interviewer. Interview schedules involve many of the same problems in item construction as written instruments, but the interpersonal nature of the interview allows more open-ended questions and interviewer probing. One example of a probe would be simply "could you tell me more about that?"

The person using the interview must consider the social and psychological meaning for both the interviewer and the respondent, for the interview is a relationship which involves both cognitive and motivational processes. The interview seems to have a number of values over the written questionnaire (8). One is motivation; there seems to be a psychological reward in talking to an understanding interviewer. A second value of the interview is that it may be used with people who can not take a written questionnaire, people such as young children or illiterates. Third, the interview allows checking questions in an overall context. A fourth major value is that the interviewer may judge the respondent's reaction and make a decision of whether to probe or soft-pedal a particular line of questioning.

The type of interview depends on its function. Interviews can be used to diagnose one particular person or research a general population. The number of people participating, the length of contact period, and the social-psychological relationship of the interviewer and interviewee all influence particular interview relationships.

The educator analyzing use of the interview in formal research should question 1) the construction of the schedule and 2) the training and competence of the interviewers. Interviewing is an acquired skill and interviewers should have had prior training; a major source of bias in interviewing is the lack of inter-interviewer reliability.

Another major method of collecting information in research is the observation, which is centered on analysis of overt behavior. This causes fundamental problems of how and what information is collected about behavior.

Observation instruments can be grouped by those which analyze verbal behavior, non-verbal behavior, and both kinds of behavior. Each type raises the question of what to study about behavior and each faces limits upon what is gathered because it 1) focuses on only a fraction of total behavioral events and 2) it demands that information be coded.

Behavior can be studied in terms of its intent, actual practice, or effect; each focus can give a different picture of the same behavior. For example, an older, larger child is observed slapping a younger, smaller child on the back. The intent of this act may be friendliness on the part of the big child; the actual practice may be interpreted as a blow, while the effect may be to arouse anger or to hurt the small child.

Most observation is carried out by trained observers or an observation instrument such as the tape recorder or television camera. The observer can take one of four roles in studying an educational situation; he can be the visiting stranger, the attentative listener, the eager listener, or the participant-observer (9). Each role has certain values. If the observer is removed from the situation he may achieve

greater objectivity, but if he takes part in the educational situation
he also achieves several things. By interacting he can get a "feel"
of the interpersonal nature of a particular situation. He can reduce
hesitation on the part of the subject by easing into the ongoing situation. A participant-observer can also gather large amounts of general
information which may have value in future reference. Obviously,
the observation instrument can also gather large amounts of information, but it cannot interact on a personal basis.

The role of the observer determines how a record of behavior
is kept. An active participant must record feelings and observations
after a period, while the non-participant observer can use a number
of recording devices at the time that behavior is in action.

All observation faces the question of the way that observed behavior is to be classified. Systematic attempts at measuring interaction have used both signs and categories of behavior. Signs are forms
of behavior that are decided upon in advance and listed. If they are
seen during a specified time period they are checked off. Observation
of categories records behavior on scales or continuums by type.

Another question raised by observation techniques is how long
the behavior is to be studied. Instruments are available which assess
for periods of three seconds, five minutes, or an hour. The length
of time that behavior is studied also affects the extent of reactive
influence that an observer has on the studied situation. Increased
lengths of time may put a strain on both the observer's concentration
and the people being studied (*e.g.*, the observer may influence people
to act in an unrealistic or unnatural way). On the other hand, increased time spans may allow the observer to get a more complete
picture of an interpersonal situation (*e.g.*, unobtrusive factors which
only become evident over a period of time).

So far there is no specific rule for determining which observation technique is superior to others; the answer probably lies in what
is studied. Essentially, observation techniques must balance the desire
for objectivity against the need to study behavior. Educators may
raise question about what is to be observed, the unit of time, the
conceptual posture, and the actual indicators used.

A final method of gathering information in formal research is
content analysis. This method is a historical analysis of concrete
information contained in existing records. Content analysis studies
the content of communications through the symbols, such as words,
diagrams, and pictures, which make up the communication itself.
The researcher analyzes the meaning against a standard that has
been set to judge content. For instance, such an analysis might at-

tempt to learn the degree of propaganda in words contained in a specific document.

To this point, collection of information for formal research has been discussed in terms of what and how facts are gathered. A third area which is crucial in both collection and analysis of information is from *whom* the data is gathered.

Who is the information about?

A *sample* is a portion of the total population which is *assumed* to represent all members; a sample may *not* be an *actual* representation of the whole group (10). Rather, a sample is accepted as representative of the group. A person who talks to one fourth-grader and assumes all fourth-grade children act basically the same has taken a sample, though admittedly a poor one; usually educational research will not take a sample which is so obviously unrepresentative. A more normal example would be to use Miss Smith's fourth grade to infer results to all the fourth-graders in Browntown Elementary. The question to be considered is whether a particular sample is considered to represent a population simply because someone said so, or whether there are more valid reasons.

An alternative to determining the representativeness of a small group taken from all members of a population is the *random sample,* which allows members of the population to be chosen against the objective standard of mathematical probability (11). It is a necessity for the use of inferential statistics. By random selection we mean that each member of the total population has an equal chance of being chosen in the sample. An example of random selection would be to put numbers representing all fourth-graders of a school system in a hat (the children represent the total population) and drawing them one at a time to get a sample group of fourth-graders (say 10% of total number).

The equal chance for choosing would be assured by returning all drawn numbers to the hat for the next draw. If there were 200 fourth-graders in a school system, the first number drawn would represent a child with one in 200 chances of being selected. If the first number was not returned to the hat, the next number selected would represent someone with one chance in 199, and so on.

Of course, most educational researchers do not rely on a hat to draw random samples; tables of random numbers have been statistically produced for the researcher to use. The tables are constructed on one fundamental criterion; that there is no "law" or explanation for the way the numbers are ordered and placed in the table. By looking at one number or a sequence of numbers it is impossible to predict a pattern. Rand Corporation created a table of one million random numbers and most statistical textbooks have similar tables of random numbers (12).

It is important that users of educational research carefully distinguish if a particular study collects data from a population, a sample, or a random sample. It is obvious that interpretation and generalization of the results to larger groups rests on the people in the original study.

There is another reason that researchers attempt to randomize samples whenever possible. Most educational research deals with situations where certain factors are not known. It is likely that no one will ever know all the things that influence a person's behavior. The same is true for all the aspects of organizations of people. Random sampling is called upon to compensate for the possibility of unknown factors entering a research situation. The reason for using randomization to control for unknown factors is simple; if every member of the total population has an equal chance of being chosen for a sample the particular qualities of one person will be counterbalanced by opposite qualities of other people. For example, random selection of teachers will, in the long run, counterbalance good with bad teachers, males with females, redheads with blondes, and extroverts with introverts.

The practitioner may find modifications of the simple random sample which are used for a number of reasons. When the population is large or distributed over a wide geographic area a researcher may use the *cluster sample*. This sampling variation uses groups rather than individual units as the basis of randomization. The groups have some like quality which allows them to be analyzed as individual clusters.

A researcher may want to study teacher attitudes in a metropolitan school system. The size of the task is so enormous that subunits of the metropolitan area are identified. An example might be local school districts. With the cluster-sampling technique the researcher would randomly select school districts to represent the metropolitan area. Once the limited number of districts was identified the researcher would randomly select teachers within each district.

Another modification of the simple random sample is the *stratified sample* technique. There are instances when it is advisable to subdivide a population into smaller homogeneous groups to insure representation; an obvious example again is the study of large school systems. Groups within the system represent different proportions of the total school population. Teachers may make up 70%, principals 10%, and central office staff the remaining 20%. The top administration may represent less than 1% of the school system's population. To counteract the real possibility of missing key actors in the system a process of probability selection is used within the number of identified sub-groups. If 10% of the population were to be sampled, the teachers, local school administrators, and central office staff would each be identified according to this criterion, a procedure that increases the precision of estimates.

Naturally, both cluster and stratified sampling affect the strict interpretation of randomization and generalization of results. The modifications change the picture of the population somewhat but the benefits in cost, preparation, and administration may outweigh the introduced bias. In these instances, researchers can predict the relationship between sample modification and strict randomness by stating a level of probable error in results.

A doubtful type of sampling which is often confused with randomization is the *available sample* or *sample of opportunity*. This is a questionable procedure because the researcher relies on whoever becomes available as his sample of a population. The man-on-the-street talk show where passersby are asked their opinion is an example. These people may or may not represent the general population of citizens. Suppose the attitudes about war were being analyzed; if a parade of veterans had just broken up it could be expected there would be undue representation of certain feelings. The same would be true if the parade had been a peace march. The sample of opportunity can be so easily influenced by innumerable factors that ordinary methods of statistical inference are not validly applicable to it.

The practitioner should also check the size of the sample in analyzing the information which is collected; generally, the larger the sample the more closely it approximates the actual population. The more people actually studied, the less chance of only one type being selected or of some other error.

While large size seems rather obvious, identifying the difference in actual populations is often difficult. Both samples and populations are made up of a number of separate, distinct units. For example, in a school system with 520 fourth-graders, there are 520 separate units or students who meet the fourth-grade classification. A researcher who drew a 10% random sample of students would select 52 children. Because the researcher defined children who happen to be in the 4th grade as his population, his sample is written n = 52.

Suppose another researcher studied the same 520 fourth-grade students, only this time the students were thought of as members of seventeen fourth-grade classrooms. The number of students remains the same, but the researcher's orientation has switched from considering separate children to considering members of classrooms as the population. In this case even if all the children were tested the total sample would be n = 17. The point is, a sample is determined *after* the population is specified. The educator should carefully consider *who* is being studied in formal research. As we saw in the example of the fourth-graders the sample taken from a student population and the sample from a classroom population may have classifications which are drastically different. The way in which samples are designated determines 1) classification of responses (as fourth-grader or as member of fourth-grade classroom) and 2) interpretation of results.

Conclusion

The collection of research information allows the practitioner a rich opportunity for intuitive analysis. Frequent questions of who, what, and how are asked in the classroom, cross the principal's desk, and are handled by the central office, and as a result, all educators are well aware of the possibility for far-reaching negative consequences when attempting to answer abstract or ambiguous questions; the same pitfalls exist in faulty research questions. The standard for judging the validity of research questions and subsequent answers rests, ultimately, in a person's logic; the reasonableness of an item, instrument, or sampling procedure depends on the rationale of the researcher. The inability to make sense or give a logical explanation of the who, what, or how is sufficient grounds for serious doubt about a particular piece of research.

Questions

1. What is an information indicator in formal research?
2. What are the different forms of information collection?

3. What are the strengths and weaknesses of written instruments?
4. What are the advantages of an interview over a questionnaire?
5. What are the possible roles which an observer may take to study a situation?
6. How does the observation technique address the balance between objectivity and human behavior?
7. What is content analysis?
8. How does a sample differ from a population?
9. What are a random sample, a cluster sample, a stratified sample, and a sample of opportunity?

10

Analyzing Information

It seems a fact of life that most formal research information is found in numerical form. Some people have an aversion to numbers and are much more comfortable with words and verbal statements. Numbers can seem confusing and may cause mental blocks; we may be familiar with discussions about a "roomful of children" but feel uncomfortable to hear the same group discussed as "N = 30."

Numbers can be thought of as just another type of symbol for reality. In many cases, a word is no closer to reality than is a number symbol; "hostility" may mean no more than "3" in the actual representation of a person's attitude. If the practitioner begins to think of numbers as another form of symbolism, the analysis of research information will not seem so complex. A picture of the relation between number symbols and the actual world of education is given in figure 19.

Figure 19

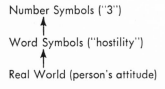

The process of assigning numbers to the real world is called *measurement*. Numbers are assigned to what is being studied according to certain rules (1). Notice how measurement "fits" with classification of the real world in the construction of the formal research problem. The researcher began with a general idea, and then as he conceptualized the variables and relationships to be studied, the idea became classified. *Classification* is the verbal description of what is to be studied — in this case, "hostility." The word symbols describe and classify the researcher's particular interpretation of reality. As long as the problem stays at the verbal level there is no measurement. When numbers are substituted for words the researcher is attempting to put information in more manageable form; measurement with numbers facilitates the handling of research information.

Generally numbers are more standardized in meaning than words in educational research. Once a number symbol is assigned according to a specified rule there is little misunderstanding about meaning. On the other hand, words, even with operational definitions, are subject to misinterpretation. Technically, an operationalized word and an assigned numerical symbol should be equally standardized, but realistically, researchers seem able to interpret numbers more consistently than words.

Perhaps the real difference is the ease of presentation. It seems easier to give the number 4 as representing an extreme of attitude responses that range from 1 to 4 than to remember the phrase "strongly disagree," which is ranked as more extreme than the terms disagree, agree, and strongly agree.

Numbers allow the researcher to handle large amounts of information at one time. A numerical symbol, once coded, facilitates the use of its word-symbol counterpart; a one- or two-digit number can be manipulated and compiled more easily than a three- to ten-letter word.

Finally, numbers are used to analyze information because of the availability of mathematical formulas and statistical procedures. Statistics reorder information and provide mathematical standards to analyze results, thereby allowing a systematic process of analysis to replace the researcher as the judge of results.

The relationship between numbers, the measurement process, and the real world can be illustrated. This has been done in figure 20.

In this illustration, notice the interrelationship between the process of measurement and that of interpretation. In effect, measurement abstracts to numbers and interpretation brings the numbers back to reality. This is a most crucial step to the whole formal research process because numbers do *not* always have the same meanings.

The symbol 3 in one report may have been assigned its meaning by a completely different rule than 3 in another report. There

Figure 20

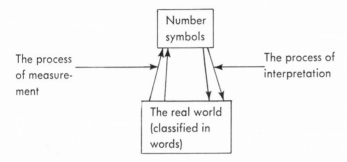

are four types of numbers in formal research which are called *scales* and which represent four levels of measurement (2). The practitioner can distinguish the different levels by identifying what a number is supposed to represent in the real world.

Nominal scales merely use numbers to *classify* objects or events into categories; numbers are used so that the researcher can identify the things being studied when the numbers are reordered. The one rule in nominal measurement is that every thing, object, or event can be a member of only one category and all members of that category must have the same characteristic.

For example, nominal scales can be set up for sex, race, color of eyes, nationality, or religion. The "exclusive and exhaustive" rule means that a person can be classified as having either blue eyes, brown eyes, or some other color of eyes, but cannot be classified in two or more categories simultaneously (3). A person with "blue-green" eyes would have to have a separate category, be classified by predominant color, or be left out of the study.

Ordinal scales use number scales to *rank* things. They add to the nominal-measurement rule by indicating that things differ in some amounts. The numbers represent things which can be ordered in relation to each other; the researcher can state that the number 3 represents an object which is "more than" 2 but "less than" 4. The rule in ordinal scaling is that the researcher cannot state *how much* less or greater one number is than another; in other words, there is no standardized scale of numerical values which objects can be judged against. An example of ordinal measurement might be three children running a foot race on an unmarked field: when Bill wins the race, a person could only judge that Sally was second and Jim third. There could be no accurate measure of how far the other two children were from Bill, and therefore any number symbols would only indicate relative positions.

Interval scales include an addition to the nominal and ordinal properties. As well as classifying and ranking there is an assumption of a standardized *equal-distance measure*. Equal distance means that the real world being measured can be analyzed on a standardized numerical scale. The number symbols have identifiable quantities and can be added to or subtracted from one another in a meaningful way. In our example of the three children, if the race had been on a marked field with yards indicated, the relative positions of Bill, Sally, and Jim could have been measured by intervals; when Bill finished, Sally had run 89 yards and Jim 76 yards. The number symbols indicated a standardized unit of measure. This means that the distance between the 92d and 94th yard line is the same as the distance between the 36th and 38th yard lines. However, the example of the children's race may be misleading in the sense that interval scales have no zero yard line; a clinical thermometer is a better example in that a living person never has a zero temperature.

The last type of scale is the *ratio*. Ratio scales classify, rank, and place equal intervals between number symbols. In addition, ratio scales have an absolute or natural *zero*; because of this, the researcher can use the scale to analyze a real object that has none of the property being measured. Returning to the example of the race, if the field was 100 yards long it would have a natural point where a researcher could actually judge zero; if Sam refused to race he would be measured at zero yards when Bill finished. Interval scales assume that all people would actually be in the race while ratio scales allow some people not to race and still be analyzed.

When numbers follow the rules of ratio scales the researcher can add, subtract, multiply, and divide them.

It is important to recognize differences in scales and their particular rules for several reasons. First, each type of number symbol represents different assumptions about the real world, and the practitioner can judge if it is logical to use a particular number symbol to indicate that world. For example, is an attitude of "hostility" more realistic when represented by ordinal or interval numbers?

Second, the type of number symbols used will determine the specific process of measurement, that is, the type of statistics used in formal research analysis. At this point we should turn back to the section on statistics in Chapter 6 to refresh ourselves on the distinction between parametric and nonparametric statistics. In strict interpretation, parametric statistics can only be used with assumed-interval or ratio-scale numbers. In recent years, however, there has been considerable use of parametric techniques to analyze research problems which actually meet ordinal rules (4). The reason is obvious; most educational or social variables do not have equal intervals or absolute zeros. For example, intelligence is usually measured on an interval scale, but is it realistic to think that the difference between 90-100 I.Q. is the same as the difference between 140 and 150, or between 60 and 70 I.Q.? Of course not. Intelligence is even discussed as a ratio scale with an absolute zero. Could a person realistically have zero intelligence and be alive?

In spite of the obvious break from reality, many educational researchers state that the assumptions of interval or ratio numbers can be used even when the real world actually gives ordinal or nominal measurements (5). The basis of the argument is that the researcher compensates for the technical misuse of number symbols in the interpretation of results (6). For example, attitudes might be treated as interval-scale measures rather than simple ranking (Ordinal) numbers so that parametric analysis could be performed; after measurement, the researcher's interpretation of parametric results would consciously remove the error of considering numbers as equal intervals. Theoretically, this approach in social science research makes sense because it lets us analyze information with the most powerful statistical tools. In practice, however, it has proved to be one of the greatest danger points in educational research; many unsophisticated researchers get so enamored with their parametric results that they forget to translate the numerical meanings back toward reality.

In either case, the relationship between the meaning of number symbols and the process of measurement used in analysis gives the practicing educator a most valuable check point for intuitive analysis. If numbers are used in ways which ignore their relationship with reality then the practitioner should find a deliberate recognition of this fact in the analysis of the results.

Univariate statistical measures

Statistics is the process of numerical analysis in formal research. Consequently, statistical techniques are basic tools used by researchers. In chapter 6, we identified the differences between descriptive and inferential, parametric and non-parametric statistics. Based on that initial discussion, we now go on to the different measures found in formal research (7).

Research measurement can be divided into two types, that which is used to describe results and that which is used for inference (8).

Descriptive statistics

Practitioners may find statistics used to describe a research situation and to analyze numerical information for measurement of:
1. Central tendency
2. Relative positions
3. Dispersion
4. Relationships

These measures compare the number scores of a study by reordering them toward one of the four objectives.

Measures of central tendency describe the middle point of a particular set of scores when the researcher wants a measure of the center score in his study. There are several types of measures of central tendency which differ in the meanings given to the number symbols. When numbers are on an interval or ratio scale, the *mean* is a common measure. The mean is simply the sum of the scores (which can be added because interval and rating numbers can be analyzed on a standardized scale) divided by the number of individuals being studied; it is the numerical average. Means are found in descriptions of research information and are used with parametric statistics.

The *median* is often used with ordinal scale numbers. This is a measure of the center of ranked data. The researcher finds the middle number where half are greater than and half are less than the number. The median is not affected by how many numbers are ranked or how extreme they are in relation to the center score.

The *mode* only measures what number symbol occurs most frequently in the gathered information. It normally is used with nominal scale numbers. If a researcher finds the number of blue-eyed, brown-eyed, and black-eyed students, the largest category would be the mode for eye color.

Descriptive statistics also measure the relative position of scores in relation to one another. The most common example of relative position is the *percentile* rank. A particular rank is a point below which a given percentage of scores fall. For example, if a student is ranked 27th in a class of 100, there are 26 students above him and 72 students below, and the student represents the 73-percentile rank

A measure of dispersion is used in descriptive statistics when some other type of information is needed to supplement the measure of central tendency. When a researcher only finds the central tendency of a group, he has no indication of the spread of scores; if he knows that a mean is 46.5, this does not tell him how far the actual numbers vary from that middle point.

Two common measures of dispersion found in formal research are the *variance* (See chapter 6) and the *standard deviation*. Both measures of dispersion are concerned with the systematic difference or spread between known scores. The variance (written s^2) is the average squared distance of individual scores from the mean. The standard deviation is simply the positive square root of the variance. The word "standard" is the tip-off that this type of measure of dispersion is used with interval or ratio number scales. The standard deviation assumes standardized scores (9). In other words, it is a measure based on the set theory of mathematical probability. If we assume a normal distribution of scores with a given mean and variance, then the term standard score refers to the distance of any *given* score from the mean in terms of standard deviations. The standard score is also called sigma (written z or T). Its importance in measurement is in reducing actual scores to common, comparable units of measure.

Finally, there are descriptive statistical measures of relationships. *Correlation* is the relationship between two sets of information which represent two variables (10). The measure of the outcome of correlation is called the coefficient. There are parametric coefficients (written r) and non-parametric coefficients (written either r_s or the Greek letter rho [ρ]) for correlations between samples. Population correlations are represented by the figure ϑ.

If there are interval scores and the assumptions are parametric, the statistical technique for correlation is called the Pearson Product Moment (11). If the correlation is based on ranked scores and non-parametric assumptions, the technique is the Spearman Rank Correlation (12).

Correlation is a popular statistic, both alone and as a lead-in to others forms of statistical analysis. Correlation asks, in effect, how do two things differ (vary) together? The statistic attempts to distinguish if there is a two-way ("co") relationship between the dependent and independent variable.

The procedure of correlation measures how close the actual scores are in relationship to one another. The relationship can range from perfectly together through no relationship to perfectly unalike.

If the relationship is perfectly positive, it will be written +1.00. This means that the relationship between the scores of the two variables stays exactly the same. When X gets greater, Y gets greater; and when X becomes less, Y does the same. Positive relationships have the X and Y varying together, up and up or down and down. The other perfect relationship is completely negative (−1.00). As the score of one variable goes up, the other goes down.

There are many possible examples of relationships between variables which can be studied by correlation. Some of them are shown in figure 21.

Figure 21

Direction of Variables	Anticipated Perfect relationship	Variables under study	
↑↑ or ↓↓	+1.00	Intelligence	School Marks
↑↑ or ↓↓	+1.00	Age of Husband	Age of Wife
?	.0	Intelligence	Body Weight
↑ ↓	−1.00	Age of Automobile	Trade-in value
↑ ↓	−1.00	Time spent in practice	Typing errors

The practicing educator should be aware that most correlation findings in education are not perfect. Consequently, the possibility of perfect correlation relationships (represented as +1.00 or −1.00) between educational variables is very slim.

If the relationship between groups of scores which represent the two studied variables is less than perfect, then researchers attempt to predict what the perfect relation would look like graphically. This is done by tracing a line on a two axis graph which fits best between the actual individual scores representing the two variables under study (13). The graph will show the individual combined number scores and the line of best fit between them. A positive correlation of about .70 would look like figure 22.

The line will slant upward and to the right, meaning that as one variable gets larger the other variable will also increase or vice versa. For example, as I.Q. increases, school marks go up and as I.Q. goes down, the other follows.

When correlation information presents a negative relationship, the line will slant upward and to the left, meaning that as one variable

Figure 22

Intelligence

School Marks

gets larger, the other will get smaller. This relationship is shown in figure 23.

Figure 23

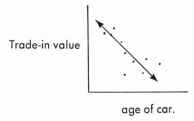

Trade-in value

age of car.

In the example, as the car gets older, the trade-in value decreases.

When a researcher finds no correlation between variables, there can be no real best-fitting line. (Technically, there is a "best fitting" line with a slope coefficient of zero). Consequently, the plotted scores would be spread randomly and show no direction, as in figure 24.

This discussion about graphs has assumed *linear* correlations. One of the greatest sources of error in educational research is that many correlation studies do *not* have linear relations (14). The line of best fit is not necessarily straight, but must curve to fit the information. A good example was our relationship between the age of a car and the trade-in value; all new-car owners know that when their car becomes one year old, the trade-in value drops drastically. This would indicate a negative relationship. However, the little old lady who bought her car new and kept it immaculate for 50 years, would have a different story to tell about trade-in value, for it drops off with car age to a certain point and then begins to rise again. There is a *curvilinear* rela-

Figure 24

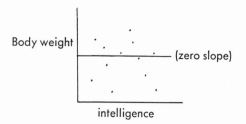

tionship if the variables are considered over a long period of time. A graphic illustration is given in figure 25.

Figure 25

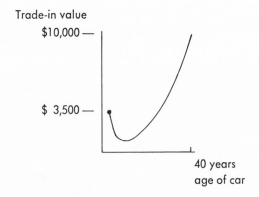

The practicing educator must check the variables under study and the assumptions made about correlation. Most research studies in education have not been made over a period of time (called longitudinal studies) or with wide samples of scores (like panel studies) (15). Consequently, correlation coefficients which show linear relationships may be false. For example, increased pupil anxiety and stress may increase productivity to a *certain point*. If a particular study only looked at relationships before that point, it might present a false picture.

Inferential statistics

Thus far the measures we have discussed have been essentially descriptive analyses of information. Research also analyzes information by measurement with built-in inference procedures which are called inferential statistics.

One such statistic, the measure of *regression,* is often discussed with correlation. Correlation is concerned with mutual relationships, but the measure of regression predicts the one-way relation of the amount of difference (variance) which an independent variable can account for in the dependent variable. Regression is an accountability technique for measuring the effects of an independent variable.

In effect, when the researcher wants to find out the *degree* to which dependent and independent variables are related, he will do correlation. Once he has identified correlated variables, his attention will probably go to predicting the *exact value* of the difference between one variable and the other (16). This prediction measure is regression.

The graphic representation of the exact prediction of perfect form is an extension of the line-of-best-fit idea that is found in the correlation graphs. With regression there are two lines for every pair of covariates. The actual statistical procedure which generates the best-fitting line in regression analysis is called the method of least squares (17).

The regression statistic needs to have interval scale numbers and both the dependent and independent variable identified. As we have seen, the practicing educator can check the use of this statistic by intuitive analysis of the researcher's logic in using numbers and setting the hypothesis.

There are many times when an educational researcher wishes to compare groups. The scores of teachers may be compared to the scores of principals on different subjects. Comparison usually is concerned with central tendency or variance.

One of the most common comparison measures of central tendencies is the *t-test,* which compares mean scores of two groups when their size is too small to assume valid normal distribution. The t-test, in effect, assumes a normal distribution between two non-normal groups by building a compensating amount of error into the statistical process and the interpretation (18). The t-test has value in educational research because it can analyze mean differences between small samples.

An extension of the t-test comparison of means is called the *analysis of variance* (written ANOVA in research literature). Analyses of variance compare differences between means when there are more than two groups. The actual question answered by ANOVA is whether the difference between the means of the various groups studied is greater than the difference between the individual scores and the mean of each group (19). In other words, the individual sample means are compared against an overall mean and, in turn, the scores within each sample are compared against their respective means. This comparison determines whether differences between samples are real or due to sampling error. The comparison of differences by ANOVA which gives a ratio of variances between and within groups is called an F-test.

An extension of the analysis of variance and regression procedures is *covariance*. Covariance is also concerned with comparison of means. In effect, the covariance procedure relies on statistical and physical control of the ongoing research process to compensate for a lack of assumptions. The covariance statistic extracts only a part of mean difference and then compares the *adjusted* means of the samples under study (20).

A statistical technique which compares groups by distribution of individual sample scores rather than by means is the *chi square* (written $\chi 2$). Chi square compares the frequency distribution of individual scores in two or more samples. Obviously, chi-square does not have to be concerned with assumptions of normal distribution. Because it compares simple frequency of scores, the chi square is particularly useful in analyzing number symbols which classify or rank people, but it can also be used with interval or ratio scales if distribution is to be analyzed rather than means.

The practicing educator can make judgments about the appropriateness of many statistical techniques without knowing the first thing about formal proofs or actual use of the procedure. The checks can be:

1. Does the analytical procedure fit the type of measurement problem under study?
2. Are the necessary assumptions for use of a particular statistic logical?

Educational research which uses the wrong type of measurement is common. The practitioner may find that a specific hypothesis will indicate comparison of sample spread or score differences but that the statistic used will analyze group means or central tendencies.

A second check can be made of the specific assumptions that a particular statistic must make. Correlation (Pearson), regression, and analysis of variance are parametric statistics. Measurement is made of various aspects *after* assumptions are made concerning the spread of score distribution, the meaning of number symbols, and in certain cases the linear relationship. Sometimes these assumptions prove to have gone beyond logic (21).

Modifications of basic statistical measures have also been developed to control many of the influencing variables. The practitioner can think of the following techniques as extensions which include larger numbers of independent variables, which add certain statistical controls, or both.

Covariance is a good example of extending the analysis- of-variance procedure to add further controls. In turn, the ANOVA technique was an extension of the t-test in order to consider larger numbers of groups. ANOVA and covariance increased the statistical analysis of educational problems but both also represent further complexity in actual analytical procedures (22).

The educator may find correlation modified to *partial correlation* and *multiple correlation*. When the researcher wants to measure relationships between more than two variables, partial correlation allows him to hold certain variables constant, in effect eliminating them from consideration, while others are analyzed. Partial correlation allows a weight of relative influence to be established for each variable in the relationship. This weighing is the basis of multiple correlation, a form of correlation that indicates how much total variation in the dependent variable can be explained by all the independent variables acting together.

Multiple Regression extends the prediction procedure so that a single dependent variable can be predicted from any number of independent variables. Where multiple correlation analyzes the degree of relationship among many variables, multiple regression predicts the exact form of the joint relationship.

Multivariate statistical measures

The realization that education rarely has research problems with a single dependent variable has led to the general use of multivariate techniques. These statistics are capable of analyzing a number of independent and dependent variables simultaneously. As could be expected, the increased ability in measurement is accompanied by increased complexity in the statistical procedure.

A multivariate statistical technique commonly used in educational research is called *factor analysis*. This is a complicated statistical procedure but it is based on a simple rationale. Factor analysis begins with information which has to be correlated; some relationship between the variables to be studied has already been found. The statistical rationale is that the mutual correlations may represent some other, more general, dimension which the studied variables share in common; there may be one underlying factor which is imperfectly measured by the variables under study.

When the educator reads about factor analysis he may find words like rotation, matrix, varimax, and loading. Rotation is a statistical technique used to help interpret results. In effect, rotation rearranges and groups numerical results so they can be most easily understood. The term varimax means that the rotation technique has reached a point where the common factors contain both high and low variables. Factor loading refers to the statistical amount by which each variable is correlated with the factor. Finally, a factor matrix is the plotting of the various loadings.

The primary use of this statistical procedure is to reduce the number of variables without losing critical information. For example, suppose a study found that the variables which measure verbal ability, friendliness, logical thinking, and ability to motivate others were all correlated. Factor analysis might find that all these variables share a common factor. If information loss is not great the researcher might want to consider the found factor (*e.g.* leadership) as representative of the diverse variables.

A note of caution

In this chapter, the coverage and explanation of measurement in research is far from complete. The statistics discussed are based on relative-frequency probabilities, which are the bases of classical statistics. We have not considered the field of Bayesian statistics which is growing in popularity (23). Bayesian statistics are developed from decision-theory models and are based on rationality in uncertain situations. The degree of uncertainty is related to circumstances at a point in time, to a person's knowledge, and to his subjective judgments. Uncertainty becomes the basis for personalistic probabilities which act as the standards for analysis. The conscious recognition of the personal values that influence statistical probabilities may prove to be a far more realistic way to analyze educational problems than classical statistical procedures, but the latter still are used in a great majority of cases.

Secondly, there of course are many exceptions to the general descriptions presented and some of the ideas can only be understood fully with much more detailed treatment than is possible in a chapter such as this one. The texts suggested for reading with chapter 5 should be studied for a real understanding of analysis.

Even realizing these limitations, the educator is far from being at the mercy of formal research. We have outlined several intuitive checks. Further, he can usually see the analysis in perspective of the total research process and this will not overestimate its single value; and as a result of our discussion of information analysis, the educator should understand enough gross differences in analysis to ask meaningful questions of those who specialize in the subject.

Questions

1. What is measurement and how does it differ from classification?
2. What are four types of scales and how do they differ from one another?
3. Statistical techniques assess numerical information in four ways. What are they?
4. What is variance?
5. What is standard deviation?
6. What is a correlation coefficient?
7. What is the line of "best" fit when a slope coefficient is zero?
8. What is the difference between a linear and curvilinear relationship?
9. What is regression?
10. What is analysis of variance and how does it differ from covariance?
11. When is the chi-square statistic used?
12. How does a univariate statistic differ from a multivariate statistic? Give an example.
13. What are Bayesian statistics?

11

Interpretation
and Conclusions

The conclusion phase of the formal research process has two important functions. First, the null hypothesis must be interpreted in a statistical manner. Second, the numerical results which were found must be re-interpreted to the real world.

We can consider assessment of the null hypothesis as interpretation at the number level. The measurement results of the research study are tested against a specific statistical standard in order to judge whether they are to be accepted or rejected (1). In other words, numerical information which has been manipulated by statistics is assessed by statistical standards.

The second level of interpretation in the conclusion phase occurs after the null hypothesis has been assessed. It is the inductive inter-

Figure 26   **Interpretation Stages**

Level 1: statistical results ⟶ statistical judgment
          (number)   (number)

Level 2: statistical judgment of   original abstract
          results ⟶   problem and theory
          (number)   (concepts)

pretation of number symbols to their real-world meanings. During this process, mathematical results are interpreted in view of the conceptual problem and of the theory which was originally set forth in the researcher's construction phase.

An illustration of the two-level interpretation process is given in figure 26.

Using the illustration of the relationship between number symbols and the real world which we considered in the preceding chapter, the two levels of interpretation can be further shown as in figure 27.

Figure 27

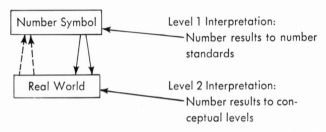

This chapter will concentrate on the different types of judgmental standards used by researchers at both levels of interpretation.

Interpreting the hypothesis

A testable null hypothesis can be identified by the type of statistics used in analysis and the grade of confidence set by the researcher. As we have seen, both these criteria are spelled out in the research design *before* the actual research study is undertaken; the construction of the null hypothesis outlines the statistic used and the level at which results are considered significant. The practitioner should check to insure that the interpretation of factual results actually follows the designated stipulations of the construction phase.

The term "degree of confidence" confuses many people who are unsure of what makes a good level of significance. This confusion is understandable because there are no hard-and-fast rules about minimum degrees of confidence; the acceptability of a particular level of significance depends on the type of problem being studied. Remember that the degree of confidence indicates to the reader the level to which the researcher is willing to accept error in his interpretations. There is always some error in inferential statistics but a level of significance can either minimize or enlarge the possibility. The researcher must make a personal judgment as to which level he will set. The practicing educator can make an intuitive analysis of the logic of a particular significance level by looking at the problem under study. The fundamental question revolves around the logic of accepting a certain chance of being wrong when making a particular decision.

If a person was placing his life on a particular judgment, how much possible error would he accept? Five chances in one hundred (.05) might be too much; even one chance of error in a hundred (.01) might be more than he would accept. He might want five chances in a thousand (.005) or even one chance in a thousand (.001) before he felt that an acceptable degree of confidence had been set (2).

On the other hand, a researcher may be studying a problem that has little personal or social implication. He may be analyzing attitudes of senior and junior high-school students about the upcoming football season. This type of problem may not force the need for a high level of confidence; the subject being measured and the consequences of a wrong decision may allow the researcher to accept ten chances in one hundred (.10) of error.

The educator will find, as a rule-of-thumb, that most educational research aims at a minimum of .05 level of significance or 95 per cent confidence in the results (3).

When a researcher must set a level of confidence for a certain problem, the decision choice involves balancing Type I against Type II errors. In a Type I error, the null hypothesis is rejected when, in reality, it is true; that is, the gamble that is inherent in his degree of confidence is lost and he comes to an incorrect conclusion. In a Type II error, the null hypothesis is accepted when in reality, it is false. Again the gamble against reality is lost. In Type I errors the tolerance for error is set too low; in Type II errors the level of significance is set too high.

This discussion may seem like a lot of doubletalk. A good example of the difference in errors, however, is demonstrated by the role of a judge in a court of law. A judge may have a reputation for being either lenient or tough. This reputation describes how the particular judge sets his standard for determining when a person is guilty.

Suppose that a judge wants to be only 90% confident that a person is guilty before convicting him. That judge's degree of confidence is set at 90%, allowing the possibility of 10 chances of error in 100; the probability would be that the judge would convict ten innocent men for every ninety guilty men. The conviction of the ten innocent men would be the Type I error. The low level of significance for guilt allows a high possibility that the prediction will not be correct.

A diagram of Type I error under these circumstances would look like this:

Actual prediction: There is a difference between guilty and non-guilty men.

Reversed Prediction (HO) : No difference between guilty and non-guilty when judge is 90% confident. This means when the judge is 90% confident, all men are considered guilty.

Accepting the Reversed Prediction: Ten out of a hundred times, innocent men will be convicted by the probability of chance alone.

If, on the other hand, the judge wants to be very sure of guilt before conviction, he may set the level of significance at .001, allowing only one chance in 1000 of convicting an innocent man. The high standard of proving guilt, however, would allow many guilty men to go free. The release of guilty men when they should be convicted is a Type II error.

A diagram of Type II error under the circumstances would look like this:

Actual Prediction: There is a difference between guilty and non-guilty men.

Reversed Prediction (HO) : No difference between guilty and non-guilty men unless the judge is 999% confident. This means only when the judge is 999% confident is a man considered guilty.

Rejecting the Reversed Prediction: Only once in 1000 times will the judge be able to determine guilt from innocence by the probability of chance alone.

Thus in the example, a Type I error would be the conviction of an innocent man while a Type II error would be the acquittal of a guilty man. This relationship is further illustrated in figure 28.

Figure 28

	Innocence	Guilt
Acquit	Acquit Innocent	Type II Error
Convict	Type I Error	Convict Guilty

Rejecting or accepting the null hypothesis

Many educators complain about the necessity of discussing the rejection of a null hypothesis. There seems to be little sense in reversing an operational hypothesis in order to test for no difference. Why not just predict a direction or difference and find if the information supports it? The answer is that rejecting a statistical standard presents a stronger case in logic and interpretation than merely accepting supporting information (4).

When a researcher studies information and verifies an operational hypothesis, one consequence is explained but others have not been ruled out. When the research prediction is left as a positive statement the researcher has no way of judging if the same information is applicable to other predictions.

For example, suppose a researcher predicted that one group of children would learn faster under teaching method A than under teaching method B, and suppose further that the research results find that the group undergoing the A method has indeed progressed faster in learning. The crucial difference between operational and null hypotheses is in how the results are interpreted. In this example could the researcher make any statements about the effects of teaching methods A and B? The A group did improve faster and the operational prediction was substantiated, but was this due to chance or to the superiority of teaching method A?

The possibility that teaching method B will be superior next time is just as good as that A will be. The equal-chance possibility will continue as long as the operational hypothesis forces comparison of methods. Each interpretation is confined to the single test between methods.

The null hypothesis interprets results in relation to a statistical standard. The difference found between methods A and B is compared to the standard of statistical probability. The researcher picks the standard by which he wants to assess the found difference; it may be five chances in 100, one chance in 100, or something else. Once the statistical standard is set, the difference between teaching methods is assessed according to the probability of a chosen level. If the results of difference are not great enough, the researcher must accept the prediction of no difference.

In effect, a null hypothesis rules out a number of other possible operational hypotheses. Information applicable to other hypotheses has the opportunity to discredit the particular reversed prediction under study. It is like the legal assumption that a person is not guilty until information conclusively shows his guilt; if the guilt is not shown, then the initial assumption of innocence remains and determines the final judgment. In research, the rejection level of the null hypothesis acts in the same manner as the theoretical legal point at which accumulated information overcomes the initial assumption that the accused is not guilty. Rejection of the null hypothesis means that all information had a chance to influence the result and that the actual outcome still was above the set standard (level of significance). The researcher can now be 95 per cent (0.5 chance of error) or 99 per cent (.01) confident that his conclusion about reality is, in fact, correct.

Directional and nondirectional testing

Standards of research may be used to predict a direction; a hypothesis may state that there will be a significant relationship between variables and, in addition, predict the direction of the relationship. On the other hand, other judgment standards in research test only for a significant relationship between variables.

In statistics, directional standards are called *one-tailed* tests while nondirectional are called *two-tailed* tests (5). The rationale for the two types of tests is easy to understand. If a researcher wishes to be 95% confident, he sets rejection of his statistical prediction (null hypothesis) at .05 level of significance. Directional testing of the prediction will assume that all five chances of finding significant difference lie in one direction; the assessment will focus on one end of the information gathered. Figure 29 represents a particular research study which is set so the hypothesis will assess only one extreme.

Figure 29   Directional Testing: One-Tailed Test

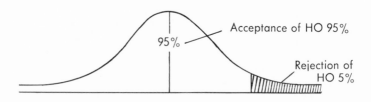

The rejection region in directional testing can be set on one "tail" of the distribution curve or the other. The critical decision which a researcher makes when using a one-tailed test is to predict the direction in which error in the null prediction may fall, and thus to maximize the size of the rejection region. The possible difficulty, of course, is that the actual error contained in the prediction may go in the other direction. There may be a significant relationship between the variables, but if the test is focussed in the wrong direction the null hypothesis will be accepted.

The nondirectional test places a rejection region on each end of the curve that represents the gathered information. In this instance, the researcher of our example must divide his five chances of reaching significance to cover each possible direction, as shown in figure 30.

Figure 30   Nondirectional Testing: Two-Tailed Test

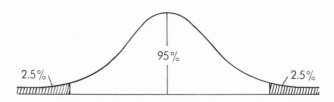

To cover the possible directions of statistical relationships, there can be only half as large a rejection region in each extreme. The possible error in two-tailed testing is that the variables which might be significantly related would not fall within the smaller rejection regions.

The practicing educator can check the statistical prediction in the construction phase to determine if the hypothesis is directional or not. The logical prediction of directional or nondirectional relationships can be an area of intuitive judgment which depends on the particular variables under study.

Statistical judgments

Chapter 10 presented a number of statistical procedures used to analyze research information. Each of these techniques has a certain standard which judges the numerical results. In some cases, the statistical standard is a mathematical table.

Statistical tables give numerical values based on certain built-in mathematical compensations (degrees of freedom, size of a sample etc.) and degrees of confidence (statistical significance). The amount of compensation is determined by a formula for each particular statistic. Number values are given for different levels of confidence which a researcher might want to put in the results; for example, if a researcher wants to set the chances of being right at 95 out of 100 times he would look for a number listed under 5% (.05) error. The specific number in the .05 column is a mathematically determined value which gives the researcher a critical number against which to check his study results. If the researcher should wish to analyze results at the .01 level of significance the table would give another numerical value. The actual means for entering a particular statistical table is explained by a number of statistical textbooks (6).

Certain types of parametric and non-parametric statistics use particular statistical tables to interpret significance. The t-test statistic is used with the *t-table;* the chi-square statistic uses the *chi-square* table; the analysis-of-variance statistic uses the *F-table.* The t-table and F-table assume normal distribution of scores and equal intervals which limit their use to parametric statistics (7). The chi-square table can be used with non-parametric statistics because the table compares simple frequency of distributions, not the "shape" of response in group (8). There also are a series of lesser known statistical tables which normally are used to assess non-parametric statistics. Some tables the practitioner may find reference to in the literature are the U-table for the Mann-Whitney test, the table for the T statistic in the Wilcoxon text, and a table to assess Spearman rank correlation (9).

When a statistical table is used as a standard of interpretation the practitioner has two options for intuitive analysis. If he knows how to enter the table the critical numerical value may be checked for the given degree of confidence. In addition, he can analyze the appropriateness of the table used for a given statistic. This second check may be difficult because many statistical techniques can be applicable when they are modified; for this analysis the educator should probably obtain expert help.

Another type of statistical standard used to analyze techniques are certain rules-of-thumb, which are based on complicated statistical rationale but which provide simple means of analyzing statistical results. Statistical rules-of-thumb help researchers to interpret meanings of correlation and factor analysis.

Practicing educators can use one such easy technique to analyze the correlation results of any study. The correlation score for any two variables tells how they relate, but the score does not tell what other differences are unaccounted for outside the two variables. For example, a study finds that achievement and IQ correlate at $r = .60$. The educator has a rough idea of the relationship on a scale varying from complete likeness to no effect. However, what does the .60 relationship say about causes of achievement difference? The indication of how much variance the two studied variables have in common is to square the result. In this example $r^2 = .36$ or a little over 35% of all difference. Thus slightly less than 65% of all difference is not accounted for. The educator should raise the question in any correlation study of how much of the total variance among variables is unaccounted for.

To summarize, the practitioner can analyze the interpretation of the null hypothesis in three ways.

1. The balance between Type I and Type II errors.
2. The choice of directional or non-directional testing.
3. The statistical standard used to assess a particular statistical technique.

These intuitive interpretations of the number world allow us to progress to the second level of the conclusion phase.

Abstracted interpretation

It is important for the educator to remember that interpreting a statistical hypothesis says nothing about the real world. The researcher who accepts or rejects the null hypothesis is interpreting numerical symbols based on mathematical rules. Likewise, the parametric statistican using interval-scale numbers analyzes the results with the same scale assumptions. In both cases, there is no need to approximate reality in the first stage of the conclusion phase.

When the measurement analysis by statistics is completed, interpretation of research results is half finished. Real-world meanings must then be reassigned to the number results and findings must be interpreted to the educational environment.

Interpretation for the real world begins with conscious recognition of the assumptions that were made in the measurement process. This recognition is particularly crucial in the use of parametric statistics. The rationale for using the more powerful type of analytical tool was based on the idea that compensation would be made in the conclusion phase for the mathematical assumptions. The practitioner should be especially aware of the need to transfer interval- or ratio-scale numbers back to nominal or ordinal realities. In most cases, the variables and relationships of the social world do not have standardized units of measure beginning at zero. If a "significant difference" is found between numbers representing attitudes, the difference between the actual attitudes must also be discussed.

Inductive interpretation

Interpretation of statistical results to the realm of education is done through inductive reasoning. Induction takes specific facts (in this case statistical results) and translates them to levels of abstraction through a logical process of generalization.

Induction is interesting because it reverses the usual association of reality with specifics. Normally, the more concrete a problem becomes the closer it is to fact. This rule still holds, but the formal-research process changes one important dimension; the construction of the basic problem sets the standard for judging reality. The construction phase, minus the null hypothesis, outlines the general explanation of reality. The idea of what is being studied is presented on three levels; if all levels are logically linked then all represent reality in the particular social situation described.

The process of measurement associated with the statistical (null) hypothesis is a conscious step away from reality. The question in inferential statistics is not whether some factual event occurred, but whether it could occur by chance alone. In effect, statistical interpretation takes the variables and relationships of the real world as givens and analyzes them against mathematical probabilities.

The numerical results of research, whether they accept or reject the mathematical prediction, must be translated back to the world of idea. In the case of formal research with consciously built deductive theory, reality is the constructed idea.

The links for inference can be the same as the "if . . . then" relations created by the deductive process. The changed operational hypothesis now becomes the "if" and the conceptual level the "then". In effect, the links between operation and explanation reverse the construction phase.

The new evidence found by a particular research study either supports or rejects a conceptual prediction about education and, in turn, an explanation of educational phenomena. In either instance, formal research is building explanatory theory—the goal of all science.

Cause and effect

One of the major problems in interpretation of results is establishing causality. In the strict sense, the actual cause of any social event can never be known. All science is directed toward presenting evidence which supports the likelihood of causality, but true causality remains an unreachable goal.

The researcher with an experimental design study can talk with more confidence about cause and effect relationships than the ex-post-facto researcher, because the experimental design allows physical manipulation of the independent variables. The researcher can actually test the isolated effect of each independent variable on the dependent variable. Suppose that a researcher wished to analyze the effect of a new teaching method on learning. In the properly controlled experiment, other intervening variables are ruled out. The teaching method becomes the "treatment" which is added to the experimental situation. When the teaching method is found to increase learning under artificially controlled conditions, the researcher can talk with some confidence about the method causing the effect on learning.

One of the major attacks on ex-post-facto research is the question of causality. When a researcher finds a relationship between variables which have already occurred, there is a very real danger in establishing one as the cause and the other the effect. Many researchers state that any attempt to establish causality under these circumstances is wrong because of the *post-hoc fallacy* (10). By this objection, they mean that a variable designated as the "cause" of a relationship between variables may be, in fact, only a symptom of the relationship. A simple example of a post-hoc fallacy could be the statement that cigarettes cause cancer. The possibility exists that glandular imbalance in an individual may cause a tendency toward cancer. The glandular imbalance may also make a person smoke cigarettes. If research focusses only on the relationship of cigarettes and cancer, establishing one as the sole cause of the other, it has ruled out the question of glandular imbalance.

However, establishing the likelihood of causal relations in ex-post-facto situations is not as hopeless as some researchers claim. Confidence in cause and effect relationships can be established logically by other techniques instead of strictly empirical means.

The ex-post-facto researcher relies on the logic of time sequence and control by third variables to assess causality. The overall logic statement is, "*if* A is the cause of B *then* A must necessarily be followed by B and if A is absent B must also be absent" (11).

The idea of time-sequence logic is demonstrated by the relationship between a lighted fuse and a bomb explosion. The researcher can distinguish that one factor preceeded the other. It would not be logical to say that because a bomb explodes a person will then light a fuse. The lighting of a fuse is more likely the cause of an explosion than vice versa.

An example of dropout and bad grades reveals the need for a second check in establishing causality. There is a need for assessment of two-way relationships by third variables. Third variables (or as many as are needed) provide a logical standard for assessment of causation between independent and dependent variables. The dependent variable is identified as the last occurring variable in the time sequence. Possible causal relations are assessed between the dependent variable and two or more independent variables. Some of the possible cause-and-effect relations are eliminated as not being logical (12). By ruling out causal relations between certain independent variables and the dependent variable there is more likelihood of causality in the remaining independent-dependent relationships.

Suppose that a researcher found an inverse relationship between grades and dropout rate; as school grades went up the likelihood of a student dropping out of school went down. Interpreting grades as "causing" dropout may be wrong because of the number of assumptions which must be made, but the causality of the relation could be put to a logical test by introducing a third variable and assessing its effect. If income of family is introduced as the third variable, the two-way relationship between grades and dropout can be checked.

Dropout is set as the dependent variable. The independent variables — grades and family income — allow ten possible causal relationships with the dependent variable (13). Among them, grades could be the sole cause of dropout, grades and income could be joint causes, income alone could cause student dropout, or there could be no relation between either of the independent variables and dropout. Logic is used to eliminate certain causal relationships from further consideration. The remaining possible relationships increase in likelihood of causality.

Reliance on elimination by other means of logic than empirical assessment still places the ex-post-facto interpretation of "cause" in question. However, even the purest experimental researcher can never reach true causality (14). The true picture presents the ex-post-facto researcher farther out on the shaky limb of interpretation but certainly not alone. All researchers who deal with the social world share the problems of determining cause and effect.

Questions

1. What are the two stages of interpretation?
2. What does degree of confidence mean?
3. What is a Type I and Type II error? How do they differ? Give a practical example.
4. What does rejection of the null hypothesis mean for the research prediction?
5. What is a two-tailed test and how does it differ from a one-tailed test?
6. What is a t-table?
7. What is inductive interpretation?
8. What is the post-hoc fallacy?

12

The Practitioner's
Use of Formal Research

The practitioner can use formal research to improve himself as an educator. It can be used to obtain a wide variety of information, to build personal theories, or to act as a guide for an actual research study carried on in the schools.

Scanning

The educator seems to work in a world where there are periods of feverish activity and then there are other periods in which there is little to do. Every good teacher, administrator, and board member will undoubtably take immediate exception to the last statement, claiming that periods of slack occur only on weekends and other times when he is not in his official educational role. A more appropriate description of the educator's world may be that there are times when he is less busy than others. During these periods of less immediacy he will attempt to clear up the amounts of written information which have accumulated on his desk. Often literature on formal research will be found among the various memos, general announcements, and other communications. The press of time may put research information at the lowest priority for consideration and first in line for shuffling to the waste basket.

Research information which finds its way to the educator's desk does not receive more time for reflection because, for one reason, the practitioner has no control over the subject. Recently, one educator had two pieces of formal research information given to him, the first dealing with the square-foot costs of building a particular school and the second describing learning disabilities of children found in a study conducted 2,000 miles away. It is natural to become impatient with the indiscriminate communication of research information that has the label of "for information only."

If the practitioner cannot control or limit the flow of research literature across his desk he can use the library; the main library of a school system or the nearby university or college library offer an opportunity for scanning. Scanning may be described as controlled searching of formal research information; the search may be undirected or directed. In undirected scanning the educator may go to several summarizing sources of research information and browse until he finds an area of interest. For example, a principal may be interested in improving his administrative abilities but not know where to go for pertinent information; the undirected scanning technique would send him to an *abstract* which reviews research on the topic of "educational administration" in three-year cycles. This beginning would allow the principal an overview of what is being done in current research about administration and would also give some guidance to specific avenues for improvement.

Scanning can also be used when the practitioner has a general idea of a subject on which he wants research information. For example, a principal or a local school faculty may want information on the effect of nongraded programs or discovery learning. In this case, the first source for scanning would be the school system's research and development department. The school system is a particularly valuable source of research information about experimental programs which have been initiated within it. A previous decision to initiate nongradedness or build "open-concept" schools on an experimental basis was probably based on specific research findings, and if so, the system could give the references and guide the beginning of the scanning operation.

If a school system does not have an R-and-D center the practitioner could begin his search for a specific topic in the library, where an *index* would give recent sources of information by topic. The educator could then go to the designated research journals.

In either undirected or directed scanning the practitioner will find the library a valuable resource. Although most educators are very familiar with use of the library, we should review three sources for finding research information. The educator should be familiar with the index, the abstract, and the *periodical* to scan for research information.

The index found in the library serves the same purpose as the index of a book. Periodical articles are listed under topics of interest. The listing includes the subject title, author, and source of the particular article. Probably the best known index for practitioners is the *Education Index* (New York: H. W. Wilson Co., 1929 to present, published monthly and cumulated by year). This index reviews approximately 200 educational periodicals and includes material on administration, curriculum, psychology, research, guidance, exceptional children, teacher education, secondary education, and many other topics.

The *Canadian Education Index* (Ottawa, Ontario: Canadian Council for Educational Research, 1965 to present) is published quarterly and indexes Canadian research by topic.

A relatively new index is the *Current Index to Journals in Education* (New York: CCM Information Corporation, 1969 to present). This source indexes by subject and author, and each month reviews over 250 different periodicals. This is an especially good source and was developed in conjunction with the U.S. Office of Education.

An annual index of doctoral dissertations with author and research method indicated is *Research Studies in Education.* (W. J. Gephart and M. Conlin, editors, Bloomington, Indiana; Phi Delta Kappa, 1953 to date).

The practitioner can also go to issue Number 13 of *Dissertation Abstracts* each year for a listing of all dissertations accepted by American and Canadian universities. Issue 13 is called *Index of American Doctoral Dissertations* (Ann Arbor, Michigan: University Microfilms, 1956 to present).

The second source that will help the practicing educator in scanning is the abstract. An abstract is a review that gives several sources by topic and a brief summary of the contents of each. One of the best abstracts of formal research is the *Review of Educational Research* (Washington, D.C.: American Educational Research Association, 1931 to present). This source reviews research findings in three-year cycles so that assessment of research developments is kept up to date. Some of the educational areas which are assessed are adult education, curriculum, planning and development, education for social disadvantaged, education organization, administration and finance, educational programs, testing, human relations in education, instructional materials, and many others.

Dissertation Abstracts (Ann Arbor, Michigan: University Microfilms, 1955 to present) is issued monthly, and lists alphabetically the doctoral dissertations accepted by over 143 colleges and universities. A brief summary of content is included with a classification by subject field, institution, and author.

Research in Education (Washington, D.C.: Office of Education, Superintendent of Documents, 1967 to present) is a monthly abstract journal about projects which are supported by the U.S. Government.

Beyond the broad abstract sources the practitioner can find many abstracts dealing with specified areas. He should ask the librarian for a listing of what is available.

Once the educator has used the index and abstract to guide the scanning process, he is ready to turn to the third source of research information, the periodicals. There are many educational publications which report research activity. Some are exclusively research-oriented while others also present feature articles; it may help the educator to browse through a number of the journals to get a feel of their particular orientations toward research in education.

It is nearly impossible to list all research-oriented periodicals which may be found in a library. Some of the educational journals which are generally research-oriented are:

American Educational Research Journal, California Journal of Educational Research, Educational Research Bulletin, Journal of Educational Measurement, Journal of Educational Research, Research in Education, Review of Educational Research.

Educational articles which present research in a feature context are most often found in the literature. Some of the better journals which carry feature-type articles are the *Canadian Education and Research Digest, Educational Administration Quarterly, Educational Leadership, Harvard Educational Review, Journal of Research and Development in Education, Phi Delta Kappan, School Review, Theory into Practice,* and *Urban Education.*

Scanning procedures, directed or not, set the stage for the use of research literature as a help in practical situations. Scanning can give the practitioner new ideas and assessments of new ideas which may help in deciding many daily questions. The educator who uses his relatively "less busy" times for scanning can improve his role as decision-maker.

Focus

A second major use of formal research is to build personal theories about educational problems. The educator does not need to accept or reject blindly what Dr. Tower of Sabertooth University said about education. Reading and intuitive analysis of formal research allows the educator to become judge and theoretician, and he probably will do the job better because he knows the specific educational problems of a particular situation. He can focus his personal theory of education in the immediate context of the school situation and thus will have a great advantage over the university professor who must generalize from some other information.

The guide for intuitive analysis of research in order to build a personal theory has been presented in chapters 5 through 11. To summarize these chapters, the educator can use the checklist in figure 31 to make judgments about formal research.

Figure 31   Practitioner's Checklist for Intuitive Analysis

I   *Overall Analysis*
_____ Are all phases and operations of the formal research process considered?
_____ Can you understand the terms and language of the articles?
_____ Could this research be replicated in your school situation?

II *Construction Phase*
_____ Can the explanation, conceptual hypothesis, operational hypothesis, and statistical (null) hypothesis be identified?
_____ Are the "if . . . then" links between levels logical?
_____ Can the dependent, independent, and control variables be identified?
_____ Can the specific relationship to be tested be identified?
_____ Does the operational hypothesis set up a prediction which
            a. has two or more variables?
            b. is directional?
            c. is testable?
_____ Does the null hypothesis
            a. list the standard for rejection?
            b. specify the statistical techniques used?

III *Carrying-out Phase*
_____ Is the research design dictated by the operational hypothesis and type of problem under study?
_____ Does the "right now" or "looking back" type of design fit the problem it represents and the information dealt with?
_____ What information is collected? Does the transfer of idea into indicator (classification) seem logical?
_____ How is information collected? Do the gathering device and procedures make sense for the type of information sought?

_____ Who is information collected from?
     a. Sample or population
     b. Randomization

_____ What number symbols are used in analysis? What scale do they actually represent?

_____ Are the statistics used parametric or non-parametric?

_____ What type of statistical relationship is used for analysis? Is it the same as stated in the operational hypothesis?

IV *Interpretation and Conclusion Phase*

_____ If parametric statistics were used, does the researcher recognize and compensate for use of interval or ratio scale?

_____ Was the assumption of normal distribution in the group(s) under study valid? Check what groups results were generalized to against the original problem.

_____ Was the level of significance logical for the type of problem under study?

_____ Did the researcher generalize to the original problem? This should be done if null hypothesis is rejected or accepted.

_____ Were results overgeneralized in light of the original problem and the actual group under study?

The checklist allows the practicing educator a standard for judging formal research. Using this standard, he can filter the research literature in areas of particular interest and acquire the competence to develop his own personal theories. Research literature can be categorized as being for or against particular concepts pertaining to crucial subjects, and the formal research upon which it reports can be analyzed intuitively. With this information the educator can build consistent and systematic explanations of educational issues.

Replication

The educator may reach the conclusion that to know if research information really fits a school situation the results must be replicated in the particular context. The third use of formal research is to set the guidelines for doing such research in the schools. Many of the studies found in educational research can be replicated in a local school, classroom, or even small-group situation. The practicing administrator or teacher can run simple research studies which meet the check of intuitive analysis. Even though they do not meet the strict requirements of formal research, replicative studies conducted in the classroom or school can indicate substantiation or rejection.

Once an area of interest has been identified by an initial replication study, the educator can set up a more sophisticated research study. The classroom teacher often will find that money is available to do research in the school if the research idea and design are well thought out and presented; many school systems will be pleased with the initiative and provide expert help. Another source of research money outside the school system that is available to practitioners is the federal government; the Small Project Regional Research Program set up by the Office of Education's Bureau of Education provides grants up to $10,000 for appropriate activities. Those who are interested in this source of funds should write to the U.S. Office of Education.

A final note

The educator who wishes to use research for practical purposes must translate it to the real world. All research creates an artificial situation. When the dependent and independent variables are filtered out for study, the artificiality begins. The same variables may be found in a school context but they will be intermingled with all other variables. The researcher's identification of a particular variable as dependent, independent, or control immediately puts it in a synthetic mold, whereas in the educational environment all variables interact, continuously forming new combinations.

Suppose an educator reads that a research study found correlation between two variables at .80 and this result is judged "highly significant." What does this say to the practitioner? Simply that in the artificial box which is created by formal research a strong relationship was found. This does not say that in the ongoing situation at Wilson High School the relationship between the same two variables will be .80. Other variables, uncontrolled in the school situation, may lower the relationship to .40 or .30. The point is, "significance" for the practitioner is not the actual number values found in formal research; they apply only to the artificial research situation.

Practical importance lies in the *meaning* of the indicated relationship. The educator in the real-life situation must translate research results in terms of meaning for practical activities.

The fact that social class and achievement are correlated at .65 by some study is not as important as the meaning of the potential relationship between differences and learning which may exist. The idea of the relationship which sets the stage for an educator's real-life analysis is the actual product of formal research.

Finally, the educator should use formal research to identify things over which he has control. Many research studies identify variables or relationships which are meaningful but beyond the power of the educator to influence.

Much of social research, for example, has arrived at one conclusion: a highly important determinant of students' achievement is the type of home they come from. No matter how meaningful this information is, there is very little the practitioner can do about the socio-economic background of students. Consequently, educators should use research to identify meaningful variables and relationships which they can *manipulate*. The relationship between teaching method and student achievement may be much lower than socio-economic status and achievement, but the teacher has control over the method. Perhaps the most important criterion for deriving usefulness from research information, yet one often overlooked, is the educator himself; in the final analysis, each individual must determine his own use of formal research.

Questions

1. What is the difference between an abstract, an index, and a periodical?
2. What indexes can be used to find information on doctoral dissertations?
3. What are three research-oriented periodicals?
4. What is the Small Project Regional Research Program?
5. What is the relationship between practical meaning and formal research?

Appendix

Directed thinking has been discussed in terms of its philosophical emphasis and political perspective in the general process of educational decision-making. The use and application of directed thinking have been identified in a broad manner, but the educator may wish a more specific illustration. Appendix A presents a hypothetical case study showing the use of directed thinking in reaching a decision about teacher accountability in a situation that makes difficult the application of rational, objective, and systematic thinking.

Principal Smith Faces the Question of Teacher Accountability
Mr. Bert Smith was recently appointed principal of Wentworth Elementary School. The three-year-old school was of open-plan design and was located in a neighborhood with rapidly changing socio-economic character. Since its beginning, Wentworth had been the source of continual conflict over the curriculum program. The previous principal had been unable to contend with various community, teacher, and central office pressures on the subject of "raising student achievement" and had resigned.

In the past month the Board of Education made several decisions about the purpose of schools and its expectations of teachers. Board members George Wilson, an engineer, was the most vocal proponent of having schools guarantee a good educational product through specification of achievement accountability and teacher responsibility. Citing Wentworth as an example of failure to meet curriculum goals, Mr. Wilson demanded that teachers be "held accountable for the achievement of children under their control." The board passed motions which demanded that the school system place a strict curriculum-accountability procedure in effect immediately, in order to hold teachers responsible for learning in the classrooms.

The local teachers' organization had resisted the accountability decisions in low-key manner, lodging a formal complaint with the national organization but giving no threat of strike or walkout. However, the board was not anxious to destroy past relations with the teachers so it asked the school system to work out an accountability system "mutually satisfactory to all people involved."

The school system responded to the board's motion by specifying that accountability was a "local school issue." Principals were required to initiate teacher accountability procedures as soon as possible. Tom Brown, the area superintendent, put it this way: "Bert, you're stepping into a hornet's nest at that school. This accountability thing has to be worked out fast. Formal accountability is the big fad now, so the board got on the bandwagon. However, they want the responsibility at the local school in case something goes wrong before election time. If teacher accountability works they'll take the credit but if it fails they have their scapegoat. I'll help you any way I can, but it's your baby. Good luck."

As Mr. Smith spent his first week in Wentworth Elementary it became quite clear that the accountability question took first priority. Monday, Bert's first day as principal, turned into a nightmare. A lunchtime social meeting with the staff became an inquisition about his stand on accountability with thinly veiled threats that implied sabotage of any assessment effort. Later that afternoon a group of community representatives, called the Committee for Better Schools, waited upon Bert and angrily demanded that the principal "weed out the bad teachers" and "teach our children the basic 3 Rs." Mr. Smith told the group he would take some type of action within a week.

That night Bert Smith thought over his first day. Although he had listened to a number of people for considerable periods of time, he knew that the information gathered consisted generally of emotional outpourings based on fear, anger, and uncertainty. He decided to spend the next three days finding out the actual situation at Wentworth. Beginning the next morning, Mr. Smith interviewed each of the twenty-six teachers on his staff. He asked each of them for 1) his definition of teacher accountability, 2) what he felt that the community, board, and central office saw as accountability, 3) whether he felt that some process of accountability would or would not work, and 4) if he would be willing to have teacher representatives "negotiate" the area of accountability. This time the gathered information still contained a high percentage of emotional responses but also some very sound factual statements. Fortunately for the principal, nineteen of the teachers agreed to "negotiate" although they wanted the arrangement for negotiations specified before they made a final commitment.

Mr. Smith spent Wednesday and Thursday contacting and talking to members of the community. The Committee for Better Schools sent three representatives. After a stormy two-hour session he obtained answers to essentially the same questions that had been asked the teachers (with an added one about their definition of teacher accountability) and a tentative agreement to sit down with a negotiating body. Mr. Smith also contacted approximately 5% of the parents of children at Wentworth and asked them for their opinions about accountability. Surprisingly, many parents felt that an accountability agreement should be worked out with the general community and that the Committee for Better Schools did *not* represent their feelings; as one parent described the committee, "they are the troublemakers trying to make names for themselves in the newspapers."

Thursday night Bert Smith called Tom Brown and explained the situation. Tom was unhappy with the idea of negotiation. "Those people may box you into some bargaining situation which will reach an agreement unacceptable to the board. If an unrealistic definition of accountability comes from the bargaining, the newspapers may blow your scheme up all over page one. If the teachers win and set the standards of assessment too low the community gripes will increase; if the Committee for Better Schools wins and accountability criteria are set too high then visa versa with the teachers."

After thanking him for the warning, Bert asked Tom for his interpretation of the central office's answers to the basic questions previously asked the teachers and community. Tom Brown gave his thoughts "off the record" but stated that he would support and defend as far as possible the local decision made at Wentworth.

Friday, Bert Smith took stock of his situation. The initial search for facts had given him enough information that he could specify three major problems to be resolved and that he knew something about potential conflicts involved in the question of accountability.

The three problems were:

1. Is the negotiation concept feasible? Will the various groups attempt to arrive at a joint decision?
2. Is the concept of teacher accountability valid? Is the assessment of teacher performance possible?
3. If accountability is a valid concept, what definition is applicable to Wentworth Elementary School?

The gathered factual information established that the teachers, the Committee for Better Schools, and the other parents had different views on teacher accountability. Each argument carried considerable merit and should, as far as possible, be made part of the final plan.

The teachers generally presented reasons that accountability procedures might be dangerous. The complexity of education makes difficult if not impossible the measurement of pupil achievement *directly* related to the influence of a single teacher. This difficulty would be particularly true in open-plan schools like Wentworth. The teachers cited several other examples of complexity. Reading is partly a function of the pupil's personality and motivation; curriculum is influenced by many factors beyond the control of the teacher; socio-economic background and family mobility are also possible intervening factors. Finally, several teachers stated that accountability involved testing and that most reading tests were culturally biased.

The Committee for Better Schools presented one major argument: children must learn how to read and do mathematics to become productive members of our technological society. They charged that the Wentworth school children were not learning these basic skills. The committee cited the Texarkana experiment in which a business firm agreed to teach students in such a manner that they would pass specified achievement tests. Why, asked the committee, couldn't Wentworth teachers function on a similar contract basis, with the results to be assessed by a battery of standardized tests?

The other parents were also deeply concerned that their children did not seem to be learning to read and to do math. These parents presented few facts to substantiate or refute their feelings about achievement; they did feel that the teachers "went overboard" on the "human growth" and that not enough time was spent on basic skills which would lead to future jobs.

Based on the defined problem and the general facts, Bert Smith made some tentative predictions about what was needed for successful resolution of the accountability question.

1. The various factions would have to agree on the idea of a mutual decision.
2. All groups would have to see the principal's role as mediator and in some instances, arbitrator of disagreement.
3. Teacher accountability would have to be accepted as a valid concept.
4. The definition of accountability must incorporate the concepts of testing and a specified frame of reference not beyond the individual teacher.

Bert also reasoned that his predictions about successful resolution were in sequential order, each hypothesis contingent upon a preceding favorable decision. He spent the weekend outlining a method by which to attack the accountability problem in a sequential fashion.

The need for a joint decision could be established if each competing faction could be made to see that it would suffer a great loss if it did not reach a mutual agreement. The one unifying interest of the teachers, committee, and parents was education of the students. To accomplish this, of course, Wentworth Elementary School had to remain open. There was some possibility that teachers throughout the city would use an arbitrary decision at Wentworth as the reason for a strike against the whole school system. The teacher organization, although currently weak, could gain considerable strength if given the right issue. Bad decision-making at Wentworth, coupled with the board's unpopular action, could provide such an issue. If the issue remained at the local school the teachers still could sabotage the concept of accountability; the school did not need to be closed for real education to stop. If the teachers were excluded from the accountability decision there was some possibility that they would lower their professional values enough to make learning a pseudo exercise. They could set, informally, a low norm for the children's achievement level. If all students exhibited the same low learning could teachers be differentiated? It would be highly unlikely that the school system would fire or transfer the whole staff simultaneously. Admittedly, the probabilities of either a teacher strike or the norm setting were remote but they emphasized the fact that the teachers must agree to any decision about accountability which would be binding upon them.

There was similar good reason why the community must be included in reaching a satisfactory decision. The Committee for Better Schools seemed quite ready to boycott Wentworth and could possibly gain enough publicity to persuade parents to keep their children away. Although the parents were against the committee as a political organization, they were in latent sympathy with its basic objectives.

In either case the risk of detrimental possibilities if there was no joint decision was too great to be ignored. Bert Smith hoped the awareness of risk would be enough to establish the need for joint decisions.

The first prediction was verified when the teachers, committee, and parent representatives sat down with the principal to "negotiate" teacher accountability at Wentworth Elementary. The actual negotiation session was preceded by an earlier meeting to decide upon an organization for the negotiations. After day-long discussions a negotiation team was established that consisted of four teachers, two committee representatives, and two parents. Bert Smith would be the chairman and would not vote except in the case of a tie.

Bert had determined in his second prediction that he would have to be accepted as mediator and tie-breaker. He established himself in this position by referring to the conditions of his administrative appointment to Wentworth. When the Wentworth principal resigned, Bert had been in his first year as vice-principal of a large elementary school. Because of his leadership abilities he was offered the job. He knew unofficially that if he resolved the controversy at Wentworth he would remain a principal; if he did not, he would not. Because of his personal commitment to the issue all groups felt that Bert Smith would fit the mediator-arbitrator role nicely. As one veteran teacher said, "If we do not resolve the accountability question it only means future confusion. Personally, I doubt if I would be touched if this negotiations idea fell apart, but our new principal sure would. It seems only fair to put him in a position where he has a chance to pull it off."

By the time Bert had verified the second prediction, the decision process had gone through Wednesday of the second week. It had taken two full days to have the groups agree 1) to negotiations, 2) to the validity of a mutually satisfactory decisions, and 3) to the principal's role as mediator-arbitrator. Decision-making on the question of teacher accountability began on Thursday.

The idea of teachers being made accountable for the achievement of children as assessed by performance fell under immediate questioning and attack Thursday morning. After several hours of discussion it was agreed that, *theoretically,* teacher accountability was a logical concept but, *practically,* teachers only partially affected student achievement. The definition of "partial" effect became the center of controversy. Bert Smith argued that none of the people involved were experts on learning determinants but that they could at least list certain observable factors which obviously affect a child's achievement. Above the objection of a parent representative, the extent of family help was decided to be one criterion beyond teacher control; the major determinant of this criterion was whether the family would or could help the child's education at home. A second criterion was the amount of mobility a child experienced during the learning process. Certainly a child who was moved from one neighborhood to another and from school to school would have his achievement in reading and mathematics affected.

The child's personality was listed as a third factor which influenced achievement, but the most bitter controversy of the day broke out over the question of which aspects of personality were outside the teachers' influence. A teacher representative argued that certain children began school with personality deficiencies which made achievement difficult. These personality problems became progressively worse as the student stayed in the school environment, until in time the child became incorrigible. When challenged by a parent about this assumption, the teacher became defensive and used the parent's child as a personal example. The result was an emotional uproar with charges and countercharges of incompetence as teacher and parent. All parties took sides and the negotiations group threatened to dissolve permanently. Bert Smith managed to regain a semblance of order by suggesting that while personality was probably an influencing factor in learning, it was beyond the capacity of Wentworth Elementary School to assess the effect objectively. Although some members of the group were still unhappy they were also pacified by this interpretation. Tempers calmed and as a result of the discussion which followed, the group recognized that accountability had at least three sets of influencing factors: 1) achievement criteria under the control of teachers, 2) outside criteria which could be observed and assessed, and 3) other factors which were impossible to judge by a local school group. Personality represented one of the "impossible to assess" factors, but its unknown effect had to be recognized in the overall evaluation scheme for teacher accountability.

A fourth factor which made student achievement difficult to assess was the cumulative effect of teachers on learning in the elementary school. In an open-plan school many students were taught by several teachers working as teams. Assessment of the effect on achievement by a single teacher under these conditions was difficult. It was decided that a possible alternative to judging a single teacher was to assess specific groups that were responsible for particular aspects of learning. This opened the question of what it is to be accountable. The teachers argued that learning was a concept with multi-faceted dimensions which contained many intangible aspects, and they cited human growth and interpersonal development as examples of these "less than objective" dimensions. The personality controversy threatened to open up again. However, the group decided to confine the question of accountability to learning of reading and mathematical skills.

Before the exhausted participants stopped for the first day, Bert Smith summarized the results of their decisions about accountability. Account-

ability of a teacher based on student achievement was a valid concept *if:*
1. it was considered theoretically.
2. it was recognized that a teachers efforts have only a partial effect on learning.
3. it was confined [for Wentworth] to reading and mathematical skill achievement.
4. it was recognized that there were three types of factors which affected achievement: those under the teacher's control, those outside the teacher's control but exercising influence, those exercising obvious influence but impossible to assess [at Wentworth].
5. the extent of family help to a child, family mobility, and the cumulative effect of teachers were considered as observable influences beyond the control of one teacher.
6. the child's personality was recognized as influencing achievement, but impossible to assess.

All members of the negotiating group voted to accept the six statements and to work within the definitions the next day.

That night Bert assessed how things were progressing. Accountability had been accepted as a valid concept by the teacher representatives. Of course, it would in time have to be accepted by the total staff, but a major hurdle had been cleared. At the same time, accountability had been limited and defined for Wentworth Elementary School. The recognition that a teacher exercised less than complete control over a student's achievement was accepted by the community. The groundwork was set so that decision-making could now focus on an actual scheme for teacher accountability. Without worrying about the future battles which would occur over the questions of testing, the blend of skill training to other forms of learning, or assessment of the observable-factor influence, Bert rolled over and went to sleep.

The next day, Friday, all participants seemed refreshed. Bert was pleased to see that group dynamics were working; the guarded-adversary roles were breaking down. People were more friendly, and the culminating incident was the public apology of the teacher who had used the personal example of the parent representative's child. The participants visibly relaxed upon that statement, and the second hard day of decision-making began.

Bert decided to press the advantage of the interpersonal climate and tackle the question of testing. The teachers had previously established a negative position toward testing, based on the argument of cultural bias inherent to tests. The Committee for Better Schools had demanded Texarkana-style standardized testing. During the initial discussion both these positions were restated. Bert suggested that the implications for assessment of student achievement be laid out for each of the positions. The teacher's view could be inferred to mean, by an extreme interpretation, that all testing must be on an individual teacher basis to insure that there was no bias in comparison; in effect, the child would become the personal standard to assess his own individual achievement. The position of the Committee for Better Schools implied standardized testing based on national norms; the child's achievement would be compared against the average for all students in the country.

After considerable discussion it was decided that neither of these extreme interpretations of testing was the best for Wentworth. The teacher's view could make achievement a self-fulfilling prophesy. Depending on who was judging the child, achievement would be interpretated as always high or always low; the expected rate of change or learning would be what the child achieved. The committee's view gave no recognition of individual or environmental differences at Wentworth school. Use of national norms of achievement would give teachers with bright children an unfair advantage over those whose students had personal learning difficulties. The most logical argument was that Wentworth represented a unique community and that achievement testing should recognize that uniqueness to some degree. Bert summarized what had been decided: assessment of achievement should be made against some standard, but both the individual child and the national norm were too extreme. The scheme for teacher accountability would set a standard somewhere in between the individual and national norms.

The question of an appropriate standard for assessment began the greatest controversy of the negotiations. The teachers wished comparison with past performances at Wentworth, but the parents and committee representatives demanded comparison at the city-wide level. The discussion made it clear that the central office's meaning, when it said that the Wentworth problem was a "local school issue" would have to be defined further. The crucial question of accountability at what educational level must be answered; was the basis of judgment to be comparison of teachers in a particular school or comparison with all teachers in the system? When the question was referred to Tom Brown, the area superintendent, he called the chief school officer for clarification. Within a hour Bert Smith and the other negotiation participants had an answer. The accountability procedure was to have, as its primary purpose, the assessment of Wentworth teachers; Wentworth school was perceived by the central office as a "test case" in the area of teacher accountability. If the idea proved to be successful there, the school system would then decide if expansion to another educational level was possible. Although it was now late Friday afternoon, Bert attempted to get a specific, mutual agreement on the question of an appropriate standard for teacher accountability. Although somewhat disgruntled, the parents agreed that Wentworth teachers would only be assessed and compared among themselves on the basis of student achievement. The meeting was terminated Friday with each member agreeing to arrive at Monday's meeting with a possible plan for accountability which incorporated all the previous decisions.

Monday of the third week found all participants still exhibiting active interest. Each person had created a plan for assessment (even the parent who could not attend that day sent one) and all were written in terms of previous decisions agreed upon by the group. The rest of Monday and all of Tuesday were spent incorporating and synthesizing the various plans into a satisfactory procedure for assessment. There were many arguments, but the negotiations team had become a real group, committed to the overall purpose of accountability. At the end of two days of intensive discussion Bert Smith could summarize four major decisions which outlined an agreed-upon accountability procedure.

First, in spite of the group's previous decision, it was impossible to classify or differentiate a child's learning ability on the basis of family help. When this concept was reconsidered as part of a specific accountability plan the group found there was no way to make a logical translation to' observable criteria. Therefore, family help was placed in the "influence but impossible to assess" category along with the child's personality.

The group decided that children could be differentiated by the extent of mobility and learning ability demonstrated on a standardized intelligence quotient test. Mobility was to be a pseudo-objective classification which would represent a joint teacher-principal decision about the effect that moving had had upon a particular child's learning. The negotiating team considered a number of alternatives before finally deciding that the combined effect of intelligence and mobility could cause a child to gain or lose up to a half year of achievement when compared to the "average" child. Consequently, the scheme to differentiate the type of child taught should compensate achievement plus or minus one-half year. A very bright child with no mobility was assumed to be one-half year ahead of the average learner and the slow child with high mobility was assumed to be one-half year behind the norm.

This meant that the child's achievement for which a teacher was accountable could be influenced up to a half year's development (plus or minus) by the *type* of child taught. A diagram of the accountability modification decided upon is shown in figure 32.

It could be expected that the vast majority of Wentworth children would have a zero compensation factor in achievement. However, the scale would help compensate the added learning difficulties or benefits that certain teachers faced in teaching reading or mathematics to a particular type of student.

A second major decision that was arrived at in two days of discussion was that teachers should not be assessed solely on the *rate* of achievement development but also the *number* of students taught. The assumption of this decision was that, other things being equal, the teacher who was responsible for the largest number of students improving the most was the best teacher in the school.

A third decision that was agreed upon after much controversy was that performances of the present teachers could *not* be compared with past performances of Wentworth school personnel. The two arguments which defeated this suggestion were that past information was insufficient to establish valid norms and that, in many cases, people would be compared against themselves. In a three-year-old school with low turnover

Figure 32   **Classifying Children Taught**

Compensation Factor in Expected Achievement:	$+\frac{1}{2}$ year	$+\frac{1}{4}$ year	0	$-\frac{1}{4}$ year	$-\frac{1}{2}$ year

Typology of Child: ←maximum learning problems   minimum learning problems→
                                                         average

IQ:	85- and	85- or	85-135	135+ or	135+ and
Mobility:	High	High	Some	None	None

the past local school achievement rates were not valid as comparison standards. It was decided to use city-wide norms of achievement in math and reading, differentiated by age level on the assumption that city scores presented by grade level could be translated into roughly comparable age-level achievement scores. There was some argument on this point and it was decided that if a teacher felt that a particular Wentworth child overlapped grade levels, the different grade level achievement norms could be averaged.

The final decision of the two days was that teachers could be assessed as individuals or as teams. For example, if three teachers felt they all influenced the reading growth of one child equally they could have the option of being assessed as a group, and their joint accountability score would be presented as an individual score for each teacher.

Wednesday, thirteen days after decision-making began, the accountability procedure for Wentworth teachers was specified. A rate of achievement would be delineated by the comparison of skill results measured by standardized tests given at the beginning and end of the school year. Teachers who taught children in more than one age level would be given separate rates of achievement for each age group.

The rate of achievement score would then be divided by the number of children in a particular age category. An average score representing both rate of achievement and number of students would be given each teacher (or group, if assessed as a group). The teacher's score would then be compared with the city norm for the particular age level. The city average would be subtracted from the teacher's average and a modified score would be obtained. Finally, a compensation factor score would be obtained from the type of students taught. This compensation score would be added or subtracted to the modified score with a resulting final teacher achievement score. This final score would be used to rank a particular teacher in order with other teachers on the faculty. Suborder rankings of teachers could be made by student age, by the skill under study, or both.

The result of the accountability procedure decided upon was a method by which to compare teachers of Wentworth in a manner which was as systematic and objective as situational realities would allow. Wednesday afternoon the negotiations group worked out two examples of the procedure's application to help "sell" it to their various constituencies. The first example was Teacher A with twenty "special" students, all seven or eight years old; nine of the children had IQs of 85 or less *and* a high mobility rating, three had a low IQ *or* high mobility rating and eight students were classified in the broad "average" category. The second example was Teacher B with a class of twenty students; seven of the students had a low IQ *or* high mobility, twelve students were average, and one student had an IQ over 135 but average mobility. Teachers A and B were compared on the teaching of reading skills over one year between pretest and post-test. The comparison is shown in figure 33.

Figure 33

Accountability Sequence	Teacher A	Teacher B
a) total grade levels improvement (pre-post test difference)	a) +6.0	a) +26.0
b) divided by number of students	b) 20	b) 20
c) average student score for pre-post test	c) +0.3	c) +1.3
d) city-wide average	d) +1.3	d) +1.1
e) modified teacher score	e) −1.0	e) +0.2
f) compensation score	*f) +5.25	†f) +1.5
g) FINAL TEACHER SCORE USED FOR ACCOUNTABILITY	g) +4.25	g) +1.70

*compensation factor for 20 teacher A students

N	compensation
9	+½ year
3	+¼ year
8	0 year
20	+5.25 years

†compensation factor for 20 teacher B students

N	compensation
7	+¼ year
12	0 year
1	−¼ year
20	+1.50 years

This example demonstrated that teacher A would be ranked ahead of teacher B in relative achievement of reading skills even though teacher B's class showed nearly four times as much gross reading improvement as the A class. The compensation factor makes the comparison of student achievement a ratio of what a student could be expected to do and what he actually accomplished.

Thursday and Friday the various representatives met with their constituencies. The teachers, the parents, and the Committee for Better Schools agreed to try the accountability procedure on a test basis only. The teachers were particularly concerned about the possible invalidity of the compensation measures. Certain parents were concerned that the whole procedure was an elaborate rationalization to justify differences in learning achievement. Bert Smith was not completely sold on the decision product but he did feel that the procedure presented a good framework for future evaluation and modification. The procedure was formally accepted by the Wentworth constituencies for a one-year trial with an established mechanism for renegotiation of particular problems.

Bert presented the plan to Tom Brown who, in turn, promoted the plan to the superintendent. A week later the Board of Education reviewed the plan and gave Wentworth a year to test this concept of teacher accountability. The initial testing of mathematical and reading achievement began while Bert Smith turned to the normal duties of the elementary school principalship.

We may have some specific objections to this hypothetical example. The final decision may not seem feasible for implementation in a real school, and the assumption that a principal, four teachers, and four community members could spend three weeks on one decision while school was in session may seem unrealistic. But the example does illustrate the process of directed thinking; it stresses objectivity, rationality, and systematic application in a real-life educational issue. In it, an educator presented with a volatile issue arrived at a decision which was defensible, testable, and capable of directing future decision-making.

Notes

Chapter 1

1. David Clark, "Educational Research and Development: The Next Decade," in *Implications for Education of Prospective Changes in Society* (Denver, Colo.: Eight State Project, 1967), chap. 10, p. 156.
2. G.T. Buswell, T.R. McConnell, A.M. Heiss, and D.M. Knoell, *Training for Educational Research* (Berkeley: Center for Study of Higher Education, 1966), p. 9.
3. Nicholas A. Fattu, "The Role of Research in Education — Present and Future," *Review of Educational Research,* XXX, No. 5 (December 1960), 411.
4. Clark, "Educational Research and Development," p. 161.
5. Dr. Nicholas Fattu, at the First Annual Phi Delta Kappa Symposium on Educational Research, Bloomington, Ind., 1960.
6. Julian C. Stanley, "Quasi-Experimentation in Educational Settings," *School Review* (Winter 1967), 343.
7. Adapted from David Clark and Egon Guba, "Effecting Change in Institutions of Higher Learning," International Intervisitation Project Address, University Council for Educational Administration, October 1966, p. 3.
8. The meaning of scientific inquiry will be discussed in Part Two of the text.
9. Generally known as phenomenological or Third-Force psychology. See Donald Syngg and Arthur Combs, *Individual Behavior* (New York: Harper & Row Publishers, 1959).

Chapter 2

1. Abraham Kaplan, *The Conduct of Inquiry* (San Francisco: Chandler Publishing Co., 1964), pp. 84-88, 97-100.
2. *Ibid.* pp. 63-65, 71-78, 100-103.

3. John R. Platt, "Strong Inference," *Science,* Vol. 146 (October 16, 1964), 347-52.

4. Charles Perry and Wesley Wildman, *The Impact of Negotiations in Public Education: The Evidence from the Schools* (Worthington, Ohio: Charles A. Jones Publishing Co., 1970), pp. 119-120.

5. William O. Stanley, *Educational and Social Integration* (New York: Columbia University Press, 1953), chap. 1.

6. Luvern Cunningham, "Collective Negotiations and the Principalship" *Theory into Practice,* Vol. 7, No. 2 (April 1968), 62-70.

7. Galen J. Saylor and William Alexander, *Curriculum Planning for Modern Schools* (New York: Holt, Rinehart & Winston, Inc., 1966).

8. Laurence Iannaccone and Frank Lutz, *Politics, Power and Policy: The Governing of Local School Districts* (Columbus, Ohio: Charles E. Merrill Publishing Co., 1970).

9. Alvin Toffler, *Future Shock* (New York: Random House, 1970).

10. Perry and Wildman, *The Impact of Negotiations in Public Education.*

11. Of course, each administrator has a different set of problems and objectives depending on his particular situation.

12. Particularly in relation to history of the "third world."

13. There are a growing number of writers who divorce the word education from the public schools. See P. Goodman, *Compulsory Miseducation; Community of Scholars* (New York: Vintage Books, 1966) or Carl Nordstrom et. al., *Society's Children: A Study of Ressentiment in Secondary School Education* (New York: Random House, 1967).

14. Chapter 3 presents six well-known philosophers who disagree on fundamental aspects of thinking.

15. PPBS is "an integrated system for providing . . . reliable information for analyzing the quality and quantity of ongoing and proposed programs and making decisions relating to these programs and their financial support." H. I. Von Haden and Jean Marie King, *Innovations in Education* (Worthington, Ohio: Charles A. Jones Publishing Co., 1971), p. 37.

Chapter 3

1. A similar presentation of competitive thinking by practical educative function is clearly demonstrated by Van Cleve Morris in chapters 14 and 15 of *Philosophy and the American School* (Boston: Houghton Mifflin Co., 1961).

2. This decision may be out of the teacher's hands. In this case, seating arrangement reflects thinking at some other level in the school system.

3. Morris, *Philosophy and the American School*, p. 414.

4. The necessity of any control mechanisms in education is being challenged from many sides: See Edgar Friedenberg, *Coming of Age in*

America (New York: Random House, 1963) or Ivan Illich, *Why We Must Abolish Schooling* CI DOC Publication 70/222.

5. Morris, *Philosophy and the American School*, p. 430.
6. Philosophy is defined as an effort to formulate a concept of the universe with the aim of understanding its ultimate nature. Horace English and Ava English, *A Comprehensive Dictionary of Psychological and Psychoanalytical Terms* (New York: David McKay Co., 1958), p. 388.
7. *The Republic,* trans. Benjamin Jowett (New York: Random House, 1956).
8. Morris, *Philosophy and the American School*, p. 329.
9. Burnet, J., *Aristotle on Education* (Cambridge: Harvard University Press, 1903).
10. *Confessions of St. Angustine,* trans. E.B. Pusey (New York: Pocket Books Inc., 1951).
11. Francis Steegmuller, *Sir Francis Bacon: The First Modern Mind* (New York: Doubleday, Doran & Co., 1930).
12. Charles Darwin, *Origin of the Species* (London: J.M. Dent & Sons Ltd., 1928).
13. John Dewey, *How We Think* (Boston: D.C. Health & Co., 1953).
14. Jean-Paul Sartre, *Existentialism,* trans. B. Frechtiman (New York: Philosophical Library, 1947).

Chapter 4

1. Ralph B. Kimbrough, *Administering Elementary Schools* (New York: The Macmillan Co., 1968), p. 66.
2. Alvin Toffler, *Future Shock* (New York: Random House, 1970).
3. Edgar L. Morphet, R.L. Johns, and T. Reller, *Educational Organization and Administration,* 2nd ed. (Englewood Cliffs, N.J.: Prentice-Hall Inc., 1967), p. 20.
4. Although legal basis for education is reserved to the states by virtue of the 10th Amendment.
5. Ralph B. Kimbrough, *Political Power and Educational Decision-Making* (Chicago: Rand McNally & Co., 1964).
6. *Ibid.,* p. 126.
7. In many U.S. communities the Bible is still read before school begins or all students engage in public prayer.
8. Eldridge Cleaver, *Soul on Ice* (New York: Dell Publishing Co., 1968), especially Section 2, "Blood of the Beast."
9. Morphet, Johns, and Reller, *Educational Organization and Administration,* p. 91.
10. Ralph B. Kimbrough, *Administering Elementary Schools*, p. 126.
11. *Ibid.,* p. 133.

12. A most famous classification of general influentials was Floyd Hunter's study of Atlanta in *Community Power Structure* (Chapel Hill: University of North Carolina Press, 1953).
13. The concept of influence by issue is identified with Robert Dahl, *Who Governs?* (New Haven: Yale University Press, 1961).
14. Laurence Iannaccone and F.W. Lutz, *Understanding Educational Organizations: A Field Study Approach* (Columbus, Ohio: Charles E. Merrill Publishing Co., 1969), p. 13.
15. Robert Dahl, *Who Governs?* pp. 226-227.

Chapter 5

1. J. Buchler, ed. *Philosophical Writings of Pierce* (New York: Dover, 1966), p. 18.
2. Adrian Dupuis, *Philosophy of Education in Historical Perspective* (Chicago: Rand McNally & Co., 1966), p. 278.
3. The labels physical and natural are used interchangeably in this presentation. Some writers distinguish between the two.
4. The artificial conditions which give rise to the name of "pure" sciences sometimes apply this label to the physical sciences.
5. Preciseness and certainty of thinking in the natural sciences is in comparison to thinking about social phenomena. Some natural science thinking, such as consideration of subatomic particles in physics, exhibit a high degree of uncertainty.

Chapter 6

1. Fred N. Kerlinger, *Foundations of Behavioral Research* (New York: Holt, Rinehart & Winston Inc., 1965), p. 32.
2. Other labels the educator may find which differentiate independent and dependent variables are active and assigned, stimulus and response, predictor and test variables. Control variables may be called intervening, extraneous, or organismic variables.
3. Paul F. Lazarsfield, "Interpretation of Statistical Relations as a Research Operation," in P. F. Lazarsfield and Morris Rosenburg, eds., *The Language of Social Research* (New York: The Free Press, 1955), pp. 115-125.
4. Researchers use the word statistic *only* when handling numerical information from a sample. The numerical measure for whole populations are called *parameters.* W.W. Wyatt and Charles Bridges, *Statistics for the Behavioral Sciences* (Boston: D.C. Heath & Co., 1967), p. 2, 221. Kerlinger, *Foundations of Behavioral Research,* p. 148.

5. Kerlinger, *Foundations of Behavioral Research,* pp. 117-145. Chapter 8 explains the rationale of probability which underlies the reason for error. Also see Hubert M. Blalock, Jr., *Social Statistics* (New York: McGraw-Hill Book Co., 1960), pp. 97-112, chapter 9.

6. There is no easy way to explain degrees of freedom. Mathematically, it is the number of elements which can vary and still fulfill requirements of the problem. This is normally applied to statistics as a means of predicting variance in sampling for a particular sample. A technical discussion of the term is found in Blalock, *Social Statistics,* pp. 156-157. Also see N. R. Draper and H. Smith, *Applied Regression Analysis* (New York: John Wiley & Sons, Inc., 1966), pp. 14-15.

7. Statistical tables list numerical values with built-in mathematical compensations for such things as number of people in a group and degrees of confidence. See Chapter 12 for further description.

8. The question of what level should represent reality is still unanswered in formal research. A good discussion of this problem is found in C. Harris, ed., "Statistical Methods" *Encyclopedia of Educational Research,* 3rd ed. (New York: The Macmillan Co., 1960), pp. 1397-1410.

9. John W. Best, *Research in Education,* 2nd ed. (Englewood Cliffs, N.J.: Prentice-Hall, Inc., 1970), p. 238.

10. Standard deviation is also called *standard error.* Blalock, *Social Statistics,* p. 136 for discussion. For testing error see Wyatt and Bridges, *Statistics for Behavioral Sciences,* pp. 66, 131, 133, 180, 209.

11. A statistical rule of thumb is that the mean for a sample containing 30 or more individuals drawn from any population is normally distributed. (Central Limit Theory). With less than 30 the normality is questionable.

12. Sidney Siegel, *Non-Parametric Statistics for the Behavioral Science* (New York: McGraw-Hill Book Co., 1965), pp. 18-26.

13. Kerlinger, *Foundations of Behavioral Research,* p. 93.

14. A good discussion of meaning is found in Abraham Kaplan's article "Definition and Specification of Meaning" in P. Lazarsfield and M. Rosenberg, eds., *The Language of Social Research* (New York: The Free Press, 1955), pp. 527-532.

Chapter 7

1. For specific examples of the problems involved see Section I. "Concepts and Indices" in Paul Lazarsfeld and Morris Rosenberg, eds., *The Language of Social Research* (New York: The Free Press, 1955), pp. 15-108.

2. Derived from the process of logic developed by Aristotle.

3. Deduction is combined with use of the hypothesis for problem construction while induction is used for problem interpretation. See M.M.

Tatsuoka and D.V. Tiedesman, "Statistics as an Aspect of Scientific Method in Research on Teaching" in N.L. Gage, ed., *Handbook of Research on Teaching* (Chicago: Rand McNally, 1963), chapter 4, pp. 142-145.

4. Fred N. Kerlinger, *Foundations of Behavioral Research* (New York: Holt, Rinehart & Winston, Inc., 1965), chapter 2, pp. 18-20. Explains the deductive reasoning in a research context.

5. W.W. Charters, Jr., "The Hypothesis is Scientific Research," mimeographed (Eugene: University of Oregon, February, 1967), pp. 1-34.

6. Kerlinger, *Foundations of Behavioral Research,* p. 11. Kerlinger also lists control and understanding as functions of theory.

7. *Ibid.* p. 15.

8. Emile Durkheim and Karl Marx are often cited as examples of building theories about social phenomena. For analysis, see Robert K. Merton, "A Paradigm for the Study of the Sociology of Knowledge" in Paul Lazarsfeld and Morris Rosenberg, eds., *The Language of Social Research* (New York: The Free Press, 1955), pp. 499-510.

9. Kerlinger, *Foundations of Behavioral Research,* p. 10.

10. John W. Best, *Research in Education,* 2nd ed. (Englewood Cliffs, N.J.: Prentice-Hall Inc., 1970), p. 270.

11. For a good example of construction analysis see Davis Kingsley, "Malthus and the Theory of Population" in Paul F. Lazarsfeld and Morris Rosenberg, ed., *The Language of Social Research* (New York: The Free Press, 1955), pp. 540-553.

12. Actual difference means within the limits of acceptable potential error.

Chapter 8

1. Fred N. Kerlinger, *Foundations of Behavioral Research* (New York: Holt, Rinehart & Winston, Inc., 1965), pp. 275-289.

2. Some naturalistic studies occur today but are not normally considered formal research.

3. Kerlinger, *Foundations of Behavioral Research,* p. 304. Randomization is necessary for the use of statistical manipulation and analysis.

4. David C. Campbell and Julian C. Stanley, *Experimental and Quasi-Experimental Designs for Research* (Chicago: Rand McNally & Co., 1963), pp. 5-6, 14, 16-22.

5. *Ibid.* Seventeen different designs are compared for external and internal validity.

6. *Ibid.,* pp. 64-70.

7. For a good description of the studies see F.J. Roethlisberger and W.J. Dickson, *Management and the Worker* (Cambridge: Harvard University Press, 1939).

8. The idea of particular statistical techniques being used more often with certain types of designs is not absolute.

Chapter 9

1. Frederick N. Kerlinger, *Foundations of Behavioral Research* (New York: Holt, Rinehart & Winston, Inc., 1965), pp. 275-276.
2. Allen H. Barton, "The Concept of Property Space in Social Research" in P. Lazarsfeld and M. Rosenberg, *The Language of Social Research* (New York: The Free Press, 1955), pp. 40-53.
3. For overall discussion, M. Brodbeck, "Logic and Scientific Method in Research or Teaching" in N.L. Gage, ed., *Handbook of Research on Teaching* (Chicago: Rand McNally & Co., 1963), chapter 2, especially pp. 75-88.
4. For example, Bob B. Brown, *The Experimental Mind in Education* (New York: Harper & Row, Publishers, 1968).
5. Kerlinger, *Foundations of Behavioral Research,* pp. 473-475.
6. For in-depth discussion see Louis Guttman, "The Principal Components of Scalable Attitudes" in P.F. Lazarsfeld, ed., *Mathematical Thinking in the Social Sciences* (Beverly Hills, Calif.: Glencoe Press, 1954).
7. Robert K. Merton and Patricia L. Kendall, "The Focussed Interview" in P.F. Lazarsfeld and Morris Rosenberg, ed., *The Language of Social Research* (New York: The Free Press, 1955), pp. 476-490.
8. *Ibid.,* pp. 484-487. Especially the discussion of range.
9. Donald M. Medley and Harold E. Mitzel, "Measuring Classroom Behavior by Systematic Observation" in N.L. Gage, ed., *Handbook of Research on Teaching* (Chicago: Rand McNally & Co., 1963), chapter 6, pp. 274-328.
10. John W. Best, *Research in Education,* 2nd ed. (Englewood Cliffs, N.J.: Prentice-Hall Inc., 1970), p. 262.
11. Hubert M. Blalock, *Social Statistics* (New York: McGraw-Hill Book Co., 1960), pp. 165-167.
12. Rand Corporation, *A Million Digits with 100,000 Normal Deviates* (New York: The Free Press, 1965).

Chapter 10

1. Frederick N. Kerlinger, *The Language of Behavioral Research* (New York: Holt, Rinehart & Winston, Inc., 1965), p. 411.

2. Stanley Siegel, *Non-parametric Statistics for the Behavioral Sciences* (New York: McGraw-Hill Book Co., 1956), pp. 21-30.
3. This rule means each category must be totally exhaustive and all categories combined must be mutually exclusive.
4. Kerlinger, *The Language of Behavioral Research,* p. 427.
5. J. Guilford, *Psychometric Methods,* 2nd ed. (New York: McGraw-Hill Book Co., 1954), chapters 8 and 9.
6. *Ibid.,* pp. 15-16. Also Sanford Labovitz, "The Assignment of Numbers to Rank Order Categories," *American Sociological Review,* Vol. 35, No. 3 (June 1970), 515-524.
7. This discussion may meet with some disagreement. Many researchers and statisticians feel that strict precision in definition and terminology is essential.
8. Robert Best, *Research in Education,* 2nd ed. (Englewood Cliffs, N.J.: Prentice-Hall Inc., 1970), pp. 225, 275.
9. *Ibid.,* pp. 267-268.
10. *Ibid.,* p. 246.
11. W.W. Wyatt and Charles Bridges, Jr., *Statistics for the Behavioral Sciences* (Boston: DC Heath & Co., 1967), pp. 193-207.
12. Stanley Siegel, *Non-parametric Statistics,* pp. 202-213.
13. Called the regression line or the line of best fit in research literature.
14. Hubert M. Blalock, *Social Statistics* (New York: McGraw-Hill Book Co., 1960), pp. 311-316.
15. A good discussion on different types of studies and their effect on research is Section III of Paul F. Lazarsfeld and Morris Rosenberg, eds., *The Language of Social Research* (New York: The Free Press, 1955), pp. 203-290.
16. Blalock, *Social Statistics,* p. 273.
17. *Ibid.,* pp. 280-283. Least squares discussion is beyond the scope of this text.
18. If perfect normal distribution is found the comparison measure is called a *Z-test* rather than t-test.
19. Called within-group and between-group variance.
20. This is a complex subject beyond the scope of this text. An excellent treatment of ANOVA and Covariance is found in W. James Popham, *Educational Statistics: Use and Interpretation* (New York: Harper & Row, Publishers, 1967), pp. 164-233.
21. There are statistical tests of various parametric assumptions. The practitioner should consult a good statistics text for tests of *homoscedasticity* (equality of variance), *goodness-of-fit* (normal distribution), and *randomness of data* (with single samples) and *linearity* (simple correlation).
22. The concept of interaction (ANOVA) and dealing with more than one interval scale and any number of nominal scales (covariance) is beyond the scope of this text.
23. I. Richard Savage, *Statistics: Uncertainty and Behavior* (Boston: Houghton Mifflin Co., 1968).

An interesting text on Bayesian statistics and their use. However, a knowledge of calculus is recommended for understanding.

Chapter 11

1. This discussion will emphasize inferential statistics.
2. A degree of confidence is another expression for level of significance. For example, 95 percent confidence equals .05 significance, 95 percent $= (1.00-.05) \times 100$.
3. John W. Best, *Research in Education,* 2nd ed. (Englewood Cliffs, N.J.: Prentice-Hall Inc., 1970), p. 270.
4. Hubert M. Blalock, *Social Statistics* (New York: McGraw-Hill Book Co., 1960), pp. 92-96.
5. *Ibid.,* pp. 122-130. A detailed discussion of the relationship between Type I and II errors and one- and two-tailed tests.
6. See the statistical textbooks listed at the end of Chapter 6.
7. Best, *Social Statistics,* pp. 275-277.
8. *Ibid.,* p. 278.
9. Sidney Seigel, *Non-parametric Statistics for the Behavioral Sciences* (New York: McGraw-Hill Book Co., 1956).
10. Frederick N. Kerlinger, *Foundations of Behavioral Research* (New York: Holt, Rinehart & Winston, Inc., 1965), pp. 359-360.
11. Blalock, *Social Statistics,* p. 337.
12. *Ibid.,* pp. 337-343.
13. Ten possible causal relationships between dropout, grades, and income of family.

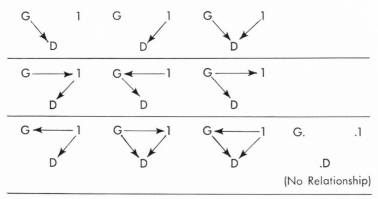

*D = dropout (dependent variable); G = grades; 1 = income of family

14. Kerlinger, *Foundations of Behavioral Research,* p. 621.

Suggested Readings

Chapter 2

Making Practical Judgments

These selections deal with the problems of making practical decisions in society. Most offer methods of thinking which highlight aspects of research thinking.

Conant, James B. *Two Modes of Thought*. New York: Simon & Schuster, Inc., 1964.

Dewey, John. *How We Think*. rev. ed. Boston: D.C. Heath & Co., 1933.

Dupuis, Adrian. *The Philosophy of Education in Historical Perspective*. Especially chaps. 10 and 11. Chicago: Rand McNally & Co., 1966.

Johnson, Wendell. *People in Quandaries*. New York: Harper & Bros., 1946.

Raup, Bruce R. et.al. *The Improvement of Practical Intelligence*. New York: Harper & Bros., 1950.

Cronbach, L.J. and Patrick Suppes, eds. *Research for Tomorrow's Schools*, pp. 14-27. New York: The Macmillan Co., 1969.

Chapter 3

1. General Coverage

Each presentation discusses the various philosophies and ways of thinking found in society and education. Each approaches the discussion from a different perspective.

Brameld, Theodore. *Philosophies of Education in Cultural Perspective*. New York: Henry Holt and Co., 1962.

Brubacher, J.S. *Modern Philosophies in Education*. New York: McGraw-Hill Book Co., 1962.

Butler, J.D. *Four Philosophies and Their Practice in Education and Religion.* New York: Harper & Bros., 1957.

Dupuis, Adrian. *Philosophy of Education in Historical Perspective.* Chicago: Rand McNally & Co., 1966.

Morris, Van Cleve. *Philosophy and the American School.* Boston: Houghton Mifflin Co., 1961.

National Society for the Study of Education
Philosophy of Education. 41st Yearbook, part I. Chicago: University of Chicago Press, 1942.
Modern Philosophies and Education. 54th Yearbook, Chicago: University of Chicago Press, 1955.

Rich, John Martin. *Humanistic Foundations of Education.* Worthington, Ohio: Charles A. Jones Publishing Co., 1971.

2. Thinking in Present Day Education

The following references show some of the specific thinking modifications which have grown out of the six competing forms. Each presents a particular viewpoint and series of practical implications for education.

a. Plato Into Idealism
Horne, Herman H. *This New Education.* New York: Abingdon Press, 1931.

b. Aristotle Into Realism
Broudy, Harry S. *Building a Philosophy of Education.* Englewood Cliffs, N.J.: Prentice-Hall Inc., 1954.

c. St. Augustine Into Perennialism
Adler, Mortimer J. "In Defense of the Philosophy of Education," chapter 5. National Society for the Study of Education. *Philosophy of Education.*
41st Yearbook, part I. Chicago: University of Chicago Press, 1942.
Maritain, Jacques. *Education at the Crossroads.* New Haven: Yale University Press, 1943.
Hutchins, Robert M. *The Conflict in Education.* New York: Harper & Bros., 1953.

d. Bacon Into Essentialism
Bestor, Arthur. *Educational Wastelands.* Urbana, Ill. University of Illinois Press, 1953.
Rickover, Hyman. *Education and Freedom.* New York: E.P. Dutton & Co., 1959.

e. Dewey Into Experimentalism
Brown, Bob B. *The Experimental Mind in Education.* New York: Harper & Row, Publishers 1968.

f. Sartre Into Existentialism
Kneller, George F. *Existentialism and Education*. New York: John Wiley
& Sons, Inc., 1958.

Chapter 4

1. The Thinking Environment

A wide variety of reflections on the environment for thinking about
educational issues.

Bennis, Warren G. and Philip E. Slater, *The Temporary Society*. New
York: Harper & Row, Publishers, 1968.

Cleaver, Eldridge. *Soul on Ice*. New York: Dell Publishing Co., 1968.

Dewey, John. *Democracy and Education*. New York: The Macmillan
Co., 1916.

Kallenbach, Warran and Harold H. Hodges, Jr., eds. *Education and
Society*. Columbus, Ohio: Charles E. Merrill Books, Inc., 1963.

Lipset, S.M. and Leo Lowenthal, eds. *Culture and Social Character: The
Work of David Reisman Revisited*. New York: Free Press of Glencoe,
1961.

Rich, John Martin. *Humanistic Foundations of Education*. Worthington,
Ohio: Charles A. Jones Publishing Company, 1971.

Skinner, B.F. *Walden Two*. New York: The Macmillan Co., 1962.

Toffler, Alvin. *Future Shock*. New York: Random House, Inc., 1970.

2. The World of Educational Politics

a. Politics in General
Iannaccone, Laurence *Politics in Education*. New York: Center for Applied Research in Education, 1967.

b. State Politics
Bailey, Stephen, et.al. *Schoolmen in Politics*. Syracuse, N.Y.: Syracuse
University Press, 1962.

Masters, Nicholas A., et.al. *State Politics and Public Schools: An Ex-
ploratory Analysis*. New York: Alfred Knopf, Inc., 1964.

c. Organizational Politics
Carlton, Patrick and Harold Goodwin, *The Collective Dilemma: Nego-
tiations in Education*. Worthington, Ohio: Charles A. Jones Publishing
Company, 1969.

Lutz, Frank W. and Joseph J. Azzarelli, *Struggle for Power in Education*. New York: Center for Applied Research in Education, 1966.

Perry, Charles and Wesley Wildman. *The Impact of Negotiations in Public Education: The Evidence from the Schools*. Worthington, Ohio: Charles A. Jones Publishing Co., 1970, especially chapter 4.

d. Community Politics

Hencley, Stephen P. and Robert S. Cahill, eds. *The Politics of Education in the Local Community*. Danville, Ill.: Interstate Printers & Publishers, Inc., 1964.

Kimbrough, Ralph B. *Political Power and Educational Decision Making*. Chicago: Rand McNally & Co., 1964.

e. School Politics

Griffiths, Daniel E., et.al. *Organizing Schools for Effective Education*. Danville, Ill.: Interstate Printers & Publishers, Inc., 1962.

Kimbrough, Ralph B. *Administering Elementary Schools*. New York: The Macmillan Co., 1968.

Lutz, Frank and Laurence Iannaccone. *Understanding Educational Organizations: A Field Study Approach*. Columbus, Ohio. Charles E. Merrill Publishing Co., 1969.

Chapter 5

The following are textbooks which deal with the methods and process of formal research in education. The practitioner may use these sources to supplement the major ideas presented in Part II.

Barnes, John B. *Educational Research for Classroom Teachers*. New York: G.P. Putnam's Sons, 1960.

Best, John W. *Research in Education*. 2nd ed. Englewood Cliffs, N.J.: Prentice-Hall, Inc., 1970.

Borg, Walter R. *Educational Research: An Introduction*. New York: David McKay Co., Inc., 1963.

Cook, David R. *A Guide to Educational Research*. Boston: Allyn & Bacon, Inc., 1965.

Courtney, E. Wayne. *Applied Research in Education*. Totowa, N.J.: Little-field Adams and Co., 1965.

Culbertson, Jack A. and Stephen P. Hencley, eds. *Educational Research: New Perspectives*. Danville, Ill.: Interstate Printers & Publishers, Inc., 1963.

Galfo, Armand J. and Earl Miller. *Interpreting Education Research*. Dubuque, Iowa: William C. Brown Co., Publishers, 1965.

Glaser, Robert, et.al. *Organization for Research and Development in Education*. Bloomington, Ind.: Phi Delta Kappa, 1966.

Good, Carter V. *Essentials of Educational Research*. New York: Appleton-Century-Crofts, 1966.

Hayman, John L. *Research in Education*. Columbus, Ohio: Charles E. Merrill Books, Inc., 1968.

Lazarsfeld, Paul F. and Sam D. Sieber. *Organizing Educational Research*. Englewood Cliffs, N.J.: Prentice-Hall, Inc., 1964.

McAshan, Hildreth H. *Elements of Educational Research*. New York: McGraw-Hill Book Co., 1963.

McGrath, G.D., James J. Jelinek, and Raymond E. Wochner. *Educational Research Methods*. New York: The Ronald Press Co.

Mouley, George J. *The Science of Educational Research*. New York: American Book Co., 1963.

Rummel, J. Francis. *An Introduction to Research Procedures in Education*. New York: Harper & Row, Publishers, 1964.

Sax, Gilbert. *Empirical Foundations of Educational Research*. Englewood Cliffs, N.J.: Prentice-Hall Inc., 1968.

Travers, Robert M.W. *An Introduction to Educational Research*. New York: The Macmillan Co., 1968.

VanDalen, Deobold B. *Understanding Educational Research*. New York: McGraw-Hill Book Co., 1966.

Wise, John E., Robert B. Nordberg, and Donald J. Reitz. *Methods of Research in Education*. Boston: Raytheon Education Co., 1967.

Chapter 6

1. General Coverage

Kerlinger, Fred N. *Foundations of Behavioral Research*. New York: Holt, Rinehart & Winston Inc., 1965.
An excellent discussion of the terms and concepts which underlie formal research in the social world.

Lazarsfeld, Paul F. and Morris Rosenberg, eds. *The Language of Social Research*. New York: The Free Press, 1955.
Provides concrete examples of the use of concepts in social fields outside of education. Also contains many worthwhile articles which explain the rationale behind research words and thinking.

2. Statistics

Best, John W. *Research in Education*. 2nd ed. Englewood Cliffs, N.J.: Prentice-Hall, 1970.

Chapters 9 and 10 give an easy-to-read overview of descriptive and inferential data analysis.

Blalock, Hubert M. *Social Statistics.* New York: McGraw-Hill Book Co., 1960.
Explains the rationale and specific techniques of descriptive and inferential (called inductive) statistics. Also compares and analyzes various parametric and non-parametric techniques.

Popham, James W. *Educational Statistics: Use and Interpretation.* New York: Harper & Row, Publishers, 1967.
Oriented toward explaining the usefulness of various statistical techniques in education.

Siegel, Stanley. *Non-Parametric Statistics for the Behavioral Sciences.* New York: McGraw-Hill Book Co., 1956.

An easy-to-read explanation of non-parametric statistics and their use in social research.

Wyatt, W.W. and Charles Bridges, *Statistics for the Behavioral Sciences.* Boston: D.C. Heath & Co., 1967.
Provides formulas and explains concrete ways to carry out parametric statistical procedures.

Chapter 9

Berelson, Bernard. *Content Analysis in Communications Research.* Glencoe, Ill.: The Free Press, 1952.

Bonney, Merle F. "Sociometric Methods" in *Encyclopedia of Educational Research,* pp. 1319-23. Edited by Chester W. Harris. New York: The Macmillan Co., 1960.

Kahn, Robert L. and Charles F. Cannell. *The Dynamics of Interviewing.* New York: John Wiley & Sons, Inc., 1957.

Kerlinger, Fred N. *The Foundations of Behavioral Research.* Part Seven, chapters 26-33. New York: Holt, Rinehart & Winston, Inc., 1965.

Merton, Robert K. and Patricia L. Kendall. "The Focussed Interview" in P.F. Lazarsfeld and Morris Rosenberg, eds. *The Language of Social Research,* pp. 476-490. New York: The Free Press, 1955.

Oppenheim, A.N. *Questionnaire Design and Attitude Measurement.* New York: Basic Books Inc., 1966.

Webb, Eugene, Donald T. Campbell, Richard D. Schwartz and Lee Sechrest. *Unobtrusive Measures: Non-reactive Research in the Social Sciences.* Chicago: Rand McNally & Co., 1966.

Index